POWER VASTU

The Great Bible of
REMEDIAL VASTU

(Including Complete Vastu Remedies for Residential, Commercial, Plots, Corporates, Factory & Industries)

By:
Vastu Guru
Dr. PANKAJ VERMA

D1666549

PREFACE

Our Ancient Vastu shastra contains information about town planning, temple vastu, great forts, palaces and residences. At that time, agriculture was the main occupation and major source of earning. But vastu's application majorly came into existence when the mass manufacturing and trading started, involving travelling and merchandise activities. Hence, focus has been shifted from agriculture to commercial and industrial establishments as a main source of income and livelihood.

But in modern context, application of Ideal Vastu has been changed to Compatible Vastu. The focus has been shifted towards space management. Where in metropolitans, spaces have begun shrinking day by day due to high cost of land and focus on ideal vastu started diminishing. From here the trend of compatible vastu started taking shape, where importance of utilizing every inch of the available space became more important than applying ideal vastu principles. To cope up with bad effects of vastu doshas and due to space management issues, remedial vastu came into picture. Ideal vastu has been replaced by compatible vastu, resulting in placemental changes according to convenience, requirements and the amount of space available in the dwelling. Hence, changing the perspective of ancient vastu shastra and its age-old occult remedies.

This shift in trend resulted in derivation of a new concept called Remedial Vastu without Demolition.

This remedial vastu focuses on best possible occult and spiritual vastu remedies used by vastu consultants. Ever rising cost of construction in metropolitans gave birth to vastu remedies without demolition, which proved to be a very powerful means for neutralizing vastu doshas. This in comparison has been proven to be more result oriented and cost-effective way, rather than demolition and re-construction of a dwelling as per ideal vastu shastra. The ease of vastu correction through Remedial Vastu has given it an edge over ideal vastu. Vastu gurus have started focusing on remedial vastu and its applications for vastu dosh correction, subsequently resulting in peaceful and harmonious living.

But owing to vast variety of healing talismans, occult items, spiritual goods and various modern tools, vastu consultants started getting confused regarding its usage and applicability. I have catapulted and projected a massive & detailed list of all types of effective vastu products and modern tools available to rectify vastu defects and doshas. These permutation and combinations of various gems, stones, rudrakshas, talismans, crystals, amulets, tools, spiritual and puja articles provide the right perception and insight into what, when & how to be used for fastest results.

It has taken more than 5 years of my research to gather and accumulate information about various types of vastu healing products and vastu correction tools. It includes their right usage, their effects, their application, directional connectivity, co-relation with each other, specific healing, multiple usage, and their availability based on actual testimonials and true feedbacks. Amassing the data, categorizing them as per their individual characteristics, features, healing powers and indexing them with the right direction and nature of vastu doshas was the most difficult part.

This book is based on behalf of my decades of practical knowledge, customer feedbacks, modern vastu shastra and compatible vastu developments, healing powers, testimonials and personal experimentations. I have provided very detailed, exact, tried and tested methods of applying these various remedies for best possible results. Every section has been provided with required remedies for incomparable effects. It's not essential to apply all the given remedies at one time. Though, minimum 9 remedies out of every list is recommendable, but applying all collectively will give best and guaranteed results. The ones marked with ^ sign are most essential and result oriented remedies. I have procured and used almost all of them. And they have given tremendous results.

This book is also an eye opener and ready reckoner for all vastu consultants and vastu practioners, who wants to get into very effective ways of vastu dosh nivaran and professional vastu practices.

I have tried to correlate all vedas, vastu tips, vastu correction and remedial vastu texts, astrology, astro-numerology, astro-color therapy, spiritual and occult mentions, yantra construction methodologies, pyramidology and crystal therapy to create an ecology of remedial and vastu dosh nivaran products. I would appreciate some serious feedbacks, viewpoints and suggestions of all vastu scholars and experts, so that we can improve ourselves in this core subject.

My valued clients have greatly admired my knowledge and understanding about the subject. They have well received and applied my suggestions, placemental changes and vastu remedies in their respective dwellings. I give full credit to my esteemed clients, my students, my close friends, my family members and my colleagues, who motivated me to write this book.

I express my special thanks to my publishers and my online partners for their valuable support and active help in successfully publishing this book.

Dr. PANKAJ VERMA
(Vedic Astrologer, Vastu Shastri, Remedy Expert & Geo-Energy Healer)
Whatsapp: +91-8882222333
Email: p.1818@yahoo.com
Web: www.vastutree.com | www.powervastu.com

FOUNDER OF:
- Bifurcating Line of Vastu
- Astro-Numerology
- Astro-Color Therapy
- Sampoorna Vastu Dosh Nivaran Kits
- Geopathic Stress Removal Vastu Kits
- Foundation Correction Vastu Kits (Neevon ki Samagri)
- Directional Healing Vastu Kits
- Specially Formulated Vastu Dosh Nivaran Directional Power Yantras

Table of Contents

Part 1

Remedies for Wrong Entrance

- Ganesh Ji Inside & Outside*
- Pakua Mirror Outside*
- Vastu Dosh Nivaran Rudraksha Yantra*^

- Antrikha / Space Stone / Space Stone Antrikha*^^
- Kale Ghodhe ki Naal^
- Secret Programmed Vastu Diviner with Gold Line*^^^ for Entrance

Remedies for Wrong Extensions, Balconies

In this section, we have provided the right vastu correction tools and vastu dosh nivaran products to be used to rectify ill effects of various extensions.

Remedies for Extension in North-East:-
- Pure Stone Pyramid
- 9 or 12 Yellow Pyramids
- Yellow Water Pyramid
- Gems & Crystals for North-East Direction:-
  - ➢ Yellow Jade
  - ➢ Yellow Aventurine
  - ➢ Yellow Jasper

- ➢ Yellow Garnet
- ➢ Conk Stone^^^
- ➢ Deep Yellow Citrine
- ➢ Yellow Triphane Gemstone^^
- ➢ Yellow Tourmaline
- ➢ Yellow Topaz
- ➢ Yellow Opal
- ➢ Oyester Pearl^^
- ➢ Moti Mani^^
- ➢ Yellow Labradorite
- ➢ Yellow Agate
- ➢ Yellow Florspar
- ➢ Yellow Spodumene
- ➢ Yellow Beryl
- ➢ Scapolite
- ➢ Samudrik Stone^^
- ➢ Golden Yellow Japanese Coral
- Directional Healing Crystal for North-East
- Secret Programmed Vastu Diviner *^^ for North-East
- Specially Formulated Vastu Dosh Nivaran Yantra for North East *^
- Water Charging Crystals
- Negativity Cleaning Crystals
- Salt Lamp
- Rudrakshas for North-East:-
  - ➢ 9 Mukhi Rudraksha
  - ➢ 12 Mukhi Rudraksha
  - ➢ 18 Mukhi Rudraksha
  - ➢ 27 Mukhi Rudraksha
- Indrajaal
- Morogul Mani^
- Conk Pearl Gilabi Mani^^^
- Yellow Color
- Antrikha / Space Stone / Space Stone Antrikha*^^^

- Nav-Grah Pyramid Yantra
- Naagmani Glowing^^
- Kamakhya Sindhoor
- Sahastra Sampudh Mani^
- Parad Shivling
- Protection Bug Fossil^^^
- Samudrik Mani^^
- Shwetark Ganpati
- Haldi ke Ganesh
- Kastoori

Remedies for Extensions in East:-

- Pure Stone Pyramid
- 5 Orange Pyramids
- Orange Water Pyramid
- Gems & Crystals for East Direction:-
  - Orange Sunstone
  - Orange Topaz
  - Orange Tourmaline
  - Orange Garnet
  - Orange Opal
  - Conk Stone^^^
  - Orange Sphalerite
  - Orange Flourite
  - Carnelian
  - Oyester Pearl^^
  - Moti Mani^^
  - Orange Agate
  - Peach Aventurine
  - Orange Beryl
  - Orange Citrine
  - Samudrik Stone^^
  - Amber
- Directional Healing Crystal for East
- Secret Programmed Vastu Diviner^^ for East

- Specially Formulated Vastu Dosh Nivaran Yantra*^ for East
- Education Tower
- Morogul Mani^
- Sahastra Sampudh Mani^
- Water Charging Crystals
- Negativity Cleaning Crystals
- Salt Lamp
- Conk Pearl Gilabi Mani^^^
- Rudrakshas for East:-
  - 5 Mukhi Rudraksha
  - 14 Mukhi Rudraksha
  - 23 Mukhi Rudraksha
- Orange Color
- Infinity Gem^^ (Faco Crystal) Green
- Sher Ka Daant (Lions Teeth)
- Junglee Suar ka Daant (Wild Pig Teeth)

Remedies for Extension in South-East:-
- Pure Stone Pyramid
- 7 Grey Pyramids
- Gemstones & Crystals for South-East:-
  - Cubic Zirconia
  - Zircon
  - Asphetic
  - Qabana Stone^^
  - White Topaz
  - White Spodumene
  - Opal
  - Triphane Gemstone^^
  - White Beryl
- Directional Healing Crystal for South-East
- Secret Programmed Vastu Diviner*^^ for South-East

- Specially Formulated Vastu Dosh Nivaran Yantra*^ for South-East
- Deep Sea Corals *(Specific Patterns Needed)**
- Deep Sea Shells *(Specific Patterns Needed)**
- Pure & Natural Crystal Balls
- White Flowers
- Boar Pearl^^^
- Negativity Cleaning Crystals
- Protection Bug Fossil^^^
- Salt Lamp
- Bidaal Mani^^^
- 925 Sterling Silver Artifacts
- Rudrakshas for South-East:-
  - 1 Mukhi Trinetra Rudraksha^^
  - 1 Mukhi Jyotir Lingum Rudraksha^^
  - 2 Mukhi Rudraksha
  - 7 Mukhi Rudraksha
  - 16 Mukhi Rudraksha
  - 20 Mukhi Rudraksha
  - 25 Mukhi Rudraksha^^
- Silver & Sparkling White Colors
- Infinity Gem^^ (Faco Crystal) White
- Kaama Siyar Singhi
- Jungli Kaali Billi ki Jer*^^
- Kamakhaya Sindhoor

Remedies for Extension in South:-
- Pure Stone Pyramid
- 8 Red Pyramids *
- Red Gemstones & Crystals for South:-
  - Carnelian
  - Red Garnet
  - Qabana Stone^^
  - Red Jasper

- ➤ Red Agate
- ➤ Red Fluorite
- ➤ Wolk Stone^^
- ➤ Red Sapphire
- ➤ Red Spinel
- ➤ Red Coral
- ➤ Heart Shaped Coral
- Directional Healing Crystal for South
- Secret Programmed Vastu Diviner^^ for South
- Specially Formulated Vastu Dosh Nivaran Yantra*^ for South
- Negativity Cleaning Crystals
- Salt Lamp
- Rudrakshas for South:-
  - ➤ 1 Mukhi Rudraksha
  - ➤ 8 Mukhi Rudraksha
  - ➤ 17 Mukhi Rudraksha
  - ➤ 19 Mukhi Rudraksha^^
  - ➤ 26 Mukhi Rudraksha^^
  - ➤ 28 Mukhi Rudraksha^^
- Red Color
- Venu Mani^^^
- Raw Burmese Ruby
- Boar Pearl^^^
- Red Lord Hanuman Photo / Idol
- Hatha Jodi Actual with Root
- Jungli Kaali Billi ki Jer*^^
- Kamakhaya Sindhoor
- Shwetark Ganpati
- Protection Bug Fossil^^^
- Gaj Mukta^^^
- Jungli Suar ka Daant
- Dakshinavarti Shankh

Remedies for Extension in South-West:-

- Pure Stone Pyramid
- 10 or 11 Brown Pyramids
- Gemstones & Crystals for South-West:-
  - Smokey Quartz
  - Bronzite
  - Brown Agates
  - Grey Agates
  - Qabana Stone^^
  - Tiger's Eye Crystal
  - Amber
  - Wolk Stone^^
  - Smokey Topaz
  - Hessonite Garnet
  - Grey Japanese Coral
- Directional Healing Crystal for South-West
- Secret Programmed Vastu Diviner^^ for South-West
- Specially Formulated Vastu Dosh Nivaran Yantra*^ for South-West
- Negativity Cleaning Crystals
- Salt Lamp
- Rudrakshas for South-West:-
  - 10 Mukhi Rudraksha
  - 11 Mukhi Rudraksha
  - 19 Mukhi Rudraksha
  - 28 Mukhi Rudraksha^^
  - 29 Mukhi Rudraksha^^
  - 1 Mukhi Trinetra Rudraksha^^
  - 1 Mukhi Jyotir Lingum Rudraksha^^
  - Charam Pashupati Nath Rudraksha^^^
- Rahu ki Kaudi
- Venu Mani^^^
- Brown & Grey Colors
- Naagmani Glowing^^
- Jungli Kaali Billi ki Jer*^^

- Hatha Jodi Jadh Samet (With Root)
- Brahmajaal
- Boar Pearl^^^
- Parad Shivling
- Shwetark Ganpati
- Talismani Mani for Enemies
- Sher ka Daant
- Shark Teeth
- Protection Bug Fossil^^^
- Gaj Mukta^^^
- Antrikha / Space Stone / Space Stone Antrikha^^^

Remedies for Extension in West:-

- Pure Stone Pyramid
- 10 or 11 Black / Blue Pyramids
- Gemstones & Crystals for West:-
  - Lapis Lazuli
  - Hematite
  - Angelite
  - Oyester Pearl^^
  - Moti Mani^^
  - Black Obsidian
  - Blue Tourmaline
  - Aquamarine
  - Blue Agate
  - Black Agate
  - Iolite
  - Conk Stone^^^
  - Sodalite
  - Blue Fluorite
  - Blue Amber
  - Azurite
  - Black Opal
  - Black Pearl
  - Black Onyx

- ➢ Black Tourmaline
- ➢ Kyanite
- ➢ Cordierite
- ➢ Samudrik Stone^^
- ➢ Purple Sapphire
- ➢ Japanese Blue Coral
- ➢ Japanese Black Coral
- ➢ Black Spinel
- Blue Water Pyramid
- Directional Healing Crystal for West
- Secret Programmed Vastu Diviner^^ for West
- Specially Formulated Vastu Dosh Nivaran Yantra*^ for West
- Water Charging Crystals
- Negativity Cleaning Crystals
- Salt Lamp
- Morogul Mani^
- Conk Pearl Gilabi Mani^^^
- Education Tower
- Rudraksha for West:-
  - ➢ 10 Mukhi Rudraksha
  - ➢ 11 Mukhi Rudraksha
  - ➢ 19 Mukhi Rudraksha
  - ➢ 28 Mukhi Rudraksha^^
  - ➢ 29 Mukhi Rudraksha^^
  - ➢ 1 Mukhi Trinetra Rudraksha^^
  - ➢ 1 Mukhi Jyotir Lingum Rudraksha^^
- Raw Sugilite Crystal
- Raw Turquoise Crystals
- Black & Blue Colors
- Infinity Gem^^ (Faco Crystal) Green
- Narmadeshwar Shivling Black
- Saam Siyar Singhi
- Jungli Kaali Billi ki Jer*^^
- Hatha Jodi
- Gaj Mukta^^^

- Dakshinavarti Shankh
- Sahastra Sampudh Mani^
- Dhan ka Bandha^
- Samudrik Mani^^

Remedies of Extension in North-West:-

- Pure Stone Pyramid
- 4 White Pyramids
- White Gemstones & Crystals for North-West:-
  - Clear Quartz
  - White Agate
  - Adra Stone^^
  - White Jade
  - Fully Round Natural Pearl^
  - Mother of Pearl
  - Moonstone
  - Triphane Gemstone^^
- Directional Healing Crystal for North-West
- Secret Programmed Vastu Diviner^^ for North-West
- Negativity Cleaning Crystals
- Salt Lamp
- Megha Mani^^
- Rudraksha for North-West:-
  - 4 Mukhi Rudraksha
  - 13 Mukhi Rudraksha
  - 22 Mukhi Rudraksha^
  - 1 Mukhi Trinetra Rudraksha^^
  - 1 Mukhi Jyotir Lingum Rudraksha^^
- Moon Rock^
- Aakash Mani Nubh Mani^^
- Infinity Gem^^ (Faco Crystal) White
- Pearl White Color
- Narmadeshwar Shivling White

- Pearl Blisters
- Bidaal Mani^^^
- Protection Bug Fossil^^^
- Siyar Singhi Joda Male Female Pair

Remedies for Extension in North:-

- Pure Stone Pyramid
- 3 or 6 Green Pyramids
- Gemstones & Crystals for North:-
  - Green Jade
  - Conk Stone^^^
  - Green Aventurine
  - Green Agate
  - Green Garnet
  - Green Tourmaline
  - Peridot
  - Hiddenite^
  - Green Amber
  - Green Turquoise
  - Malachite
  - Oyester Pearl^^
  - Moti Mani^^
  - Green Fluorite
  - Green Jasper
  - Amazonite
  - Florite
  - Samudrik Stone^^
  - Parasha Gemstone^^^
  - Green Tourmaline
  - Green Beryl^
- Green Water Pyramid
- Directional Healing Crystal for North
- Secret Programmed Vastu Diviner^^ for North
- Specially Formulated Vastu Dosh Nivaran Yantra*^ for North

- Water Charging Crystals
- Negativity Cleaning Crystals
- Salt Lamp
- Rudraksha for North:-
  - 3 Mukhi Rudraksha
  - 6 Mukhi Rudraksha
  - 15 Mukhi Rudraksha
  - 21 Mukhi Rudraksha^
  - 25 Mukhi Rudraksha^^
  - 30 Mukhi Rudraksha^^
- Money Eggs^^
- Infinity Gem^^ (Faco Crystal) Green
- Morogul Mani^
- Green Color
- Plants
- Samudrik Mani^^
- Raw Emerald
- Conk Pearl Gilabi Mani^^^
- Indrajaal, Brahmajaal
- Jungli Kaali Billi ki Jer*^^
- Hatha Jodi with Actual Root
- Saam Siyar Singhi
- Sahastra Sampudh Mani^
- Dakshinavarti Shankh
- Dhan ka Bandha*^
- Asphetic Shri Yantra

Remedies for Wrong Reductions / Cutouts

In this section, we have provided the right vastu correction tools and vastu dosh nivaran products to be used to rectify ill effects of various reductions and cutouts.

Remedies for Reduction / Cutout in North-East

- Pure Stone Pyramid
- 9 or 12 Yellow Pyramids
- Yellow Water Pyramid
- Gems & Crystals for North-East Direction:-
  - ➢ Yellow Jade
  - ➢ Yellow Aventurine
  - ➢ Yellow Jasper
  - ➢ Yellow Garnet
  - ➢ Conk Stone^^^
  - ➢ Deep Yellow Citrine
  - ➢ Yellow Triphane Gemstone^^
  - ➢ Yellow Tourmaline
  - ➢ Yellow Topaz

- ➢ Yellow Opal
- ➢ Oyester Pearl^^
- ➢ Moti Mani^^
- ➢ Yellow Labradorite
- ➢ Yellow Agate
- ➢ Yellow Florspar
- ➢ Yellow Spodumene
- ➢ Yellow Beryl
- ➢ Scapolite
- ➢ Samudrik Stone^^
- ➢ Golden Yellow Japanese Coral
- Directional Healing Crystal for North-East
- Secret Programmed Vastu Diviner *^^ for North-East
- Specially Formulated Vastu Dosh Nivaran Yantra for North East *^
- Water Charging Crystals
- Negativity Cleaning Crystals
- Salt Lamp
- Rudrakshas for North-East:-
  - ➢ 9 Mukhi Rudraksha
  - ➢ 12 Mukhi Rudraksha
  - ➢ 18 Mukhi Rudraksha
  - ➢ 27 Mukhi Rudraksha
- Indrajaal
- Morogul Mani^
- Conk Pearl Gilabi Mani^^^
- Yellow Color
- Antrikha / Space Stone / Space Stone Antrikha*^^^
- Nav-Grah Pyramid Yantra
- Naagmani Glowing^^
- Kamakhya Sindhoor
- Sahastra Sampudh Mani^
- Parad Shivling
- Samudrik Mani^^

- Protection Bug Fossil^^^
- Shwetark Ganpati
- Haldi ke Ganesh
- Kastoori

Remedies for Reduction / Cutout in East:-

- Pure Stone Pyramid
- 5 Orange Pyramids
- Orange Water Pyramid
- Gems & Crystals for East Direction:-
  - ➤ Orange Sunstone
  - ➤ Orange Topaz
  - ➤ Orange Tourmaline
  - ➤ Orange Garnet
  - ➤ Orange Opal
  - ➤ Conk Stone^^^
  - ➤ Orange Sphalerite
  - ➤ Orange Flourite
  - ➤ Carnelian
  - ➤ Oyester Pearl^^
  - ➤ Moti Mani^^
  - ➤ Orange Agate
  - ➤ Peach Aventurine
  - ➤ Orange Beryl
  - ➤ Orange Citrine
  - ➤ Samudrik Stone^^
  - ➤ Amber
- Directional Healing Crystal for East
- Secret Programmed Vastu Diviner^^ for East
- Specially Formulated Vastu Dosh Nivaran Yantra*^ for East
- Education Tower
- Morogul Mani^
- Sahastra Sampudh Mani^
- Water Charging Crystals

- Negativity Cleaning Crystals
- Salt Lamp
- Conk Pearl Gilabi Mani^^^
- Rudrakshas for East:-
  - ➢ 5 Mukhi Rudraksha
  - ➢ 14 Mukhi Rudraksha
  - ➢ 23 Mukhi Rudraksha
- Orange Color
- Infinity Gem^^ (Faco Crystal) Green
- Sher Ka Daant (Lions Teeth)
- Junglee Suar ka Daant (Wild Pig Teeth)

Remedies for Reduction / Cutout in South-East:-

- Pure Stone Pyramid
- 7 Grey Pyramids
- Gemstones & Crystals for South-East:-
  - ➢ Cubic Zirconia
  - ➢ Zircon
  - ➢ Asphetic
  - ➢ Qabana Stone^^
  - ➢ White Topaz
  - ➢ White Spodumene
  - ➢ Opal
  - ➢ Triphane Gemstone^^
  - ➢ White Beryl
- Directional Healing Crystal for South-East
- Secret Programmed Vastu Diviner*^^ for South-East
- Specially Formulated Vastu Dosh Nivaran Yantra*^ for South-East
- Deep Sea Corals *(Specific Patterns Needed)*
- Deep Sea Shells *(Specific Patterns Needed)*
- Pure & Natural Crystal Balls
- White Flowers

- Protection Bug Fossil^^^
- Boar Pearl^^^
- Negativity Cleaning Crystals
- Salt Lamp
- Bidaal Mani^^^
- 925 Sterling Silver Artifacts
- Rudrakshas for South-East:-
  ➢ 1 Mukhi Trinetra Rudraksha^^
  ➢ 1 Mukhi Jyotir Lingum Rudraksha^^
  ➢ 2 Mukhi Rudraksha
  ➢ 7 Mukhi Rudraksha
  ➢ 16 Mukhi Rudraksha
  ➢ 20 Mukhi Rudraksha
  ➢ 25 Mukhi Rudraksha^^
- Silver & Sparkling White Colors
- Infinity Gem^^ (Faco Crystal) White
- Kaama Siyar Singhi
- Jungli Kaali Billi ki Jer*^^
- Kamakhaya Sindhoor

Remedies for Reduction / Cutout in South:-
- Pure Stone Pyramid
- 8 Red Pyramids *
- Red Gemstones & Crystals for South:-
  ➢ Carnelian
  ➢ Red Garnet
  ➢ Qabana Stone^^
  ➢ Red Jasper
  ➢ Red Agate
  ➢ Red Fluorite
  ➢ Wolk Stone^^
  ➢ Red Sapphire
  ➢ Red Spinel
  ➢ Red Coral
  ➢ Heart Shaped Coral

- Directional Healing Crystal for South
- Secret Programmed Vastu Diviner^^ for South
- Specially Formulated Vastu Dosh Nivaran Yantra*^ for South
- Negativity Cleaning Crystals
- Salt Lamp
- Rudrakshas for South:-
  - ➢ 1 Mukhi Rudraksha
  - ➢ 8 Mukhi Rudraksha
  - ➢ 17 Mukhi Rudraksha
  - ➢ 19 Mukhi Rudraksha^^
  - ➢ 26 Mukhi Rudraksha^^
  - ➢ 28 Mukhi Rudraksha^^
- Red Color
- Venu Mani^^^
- Protection Bug Fossil^^^
- Raw Burmese Ruby
- Boar Pearl^^^
- Red Lord Hanuman Photo / Idol
- Hatha Jodi Actual with Root
- Jungli Kaali Billi ki Jer*^^
- Kamakhaya Sindhoor
- Shwetark Ganpati
- Gaj Mukta^^^
- Jungli Suar ka Daant
- Dakshinavarti Shankh

Remedies for Reduction / Cutout in South-West:-
- Pure Stone Pyramid
- 10 or 11 Brown Pyramids
- Gemstones & Crystals for South-West:-
  - ➢ Smokey Quartz
  - ➢ Bronzite
  - ➢ Brown Agates

- ➢ Grey Agates
- ➢ Qabana Stone^^
- ➢ Tiger's Eye Crystal
- ➢ Amber
- ➢ Wolk Stone^^
- ➢ Smokey Topaz
- ➢ Hessonite Garnet
- ➢ Grey Japanese Coral
- Directional Healing Crystal for South-West
- Secret Programmed Vastu Diviner^^ for South-West
- Specially Formulated Vastu Dosh Nivaran Yantra*^ for South-West
- Negativity Cleaning Crystals
- Salt Lamp
- Rudrakshas for South-West:-
  - ➢ 10 Mukhi Rudraksha
  - ➢ 11 Mukhi Rudraksha
  - ➢ 19 Mukhi Rudraksha
  - ➢ 28 Mukhi Rudraksha^^
  - ➢ 29 Mukhi Rudraksha^^
  - ➢ 1 Mukhi Trinetra Rudraksha^^
  - ➢ 1 Mukhi Jyotir Lingum Rudraksha^^
  - ➢ Charam Pashupati Nath Rudraksha^^^
- Rahu ki Kaudi
- Venu Mani^^^
- Protection Bug Fossil^^^
- Brown & Grey Colors
- Naagmani Glowing^^
- Jungli Kaali Billi ki Jer*^^
- Hatha Jodi Jadh Samet (With Root)
- Brahmajaal
- Boar Pearl^^^
- Parad Shivling
- Shwetark Ganpati
- Talismani Mani for Enemies

- Sher ka Daant
- Shark Teeth
- Gaj Mukta^^^
- Antrikha / Space Stone / Space Stone Antrikha^^^

Remedies for Reduction / Cutout in West:-

- Pure Stone Pyramid
- 10 or 11 Black / Blue Pyramids
- Gemstones & Crystals for West:-
  - Lapis Lazuli
  - Hematite
  - Angelite
  - Oyester Pearl^^
  - Moti Mani^^
  - Black Obsidian
  - Blue Tourmaline
  - Aquamarine
  - Blue Agate
  - Black Agate
  - Iolite
  - Conk Stone^^^
  - Sodalite
  - Blue Fluorite
  - Blue Amber
  - Azurite
  - Black Opal
  - Black Pearl
  - Black Onyx
  - Black Tourmaline
  - Kyanite
  - Cordierite
  - Samudrik Stone^^
  - Purple Sapphire
  - Japanese Blue Coral
  - Japanese Black Coral
  - Black Spinel

- Blue Water Pyramid
- Directional Healing Crystal for West
- Secret Programmed Vastu Diviner^^ for West
- Specially Formulated Vastu Dosh Nivaran Yantra*^ for West
- Water Charging Crystals
- Negativity Cleaning Crystals
- Salt Lamp
- Morogul Mani^
- Conk Pearl Gilabi Mani^^^
- Education Tower
- Rudraksha for West:-
  - 10 Mukhi Rudraksha
  - 11 Mukhi Rudraksha
  - 19 Mukhi Rudraksha
  - 28 Mukhi Rudraksha^^
  - 29 Mukhi Rudraksha^^
  - 1 Mukhi Trinetra Rudraksha^^
  - 1 Mukhi Jyotir Lingum Rudraksha^^
- Raw Sugilite Crystal
- Raw Turquoise Crystals
- Black & Blue Colors
- Infinity Gem^^ (Faco Crystal) Green
- Narmadeshwar Shivling Black
- Saam Siyar Singhi
- Jungli Kaali Billi ki Jer*^^
- Hatha Jodi
- Gaj Mukta^^^
- Dakshinavarti Shankh
- Sahastra Sampudh Mani^
- Dhan ka Bandha^
- Samudrik Mani^^

Remedies for Reduction / Cutout in North-West:-

- Pure Stone Pyramid
- 4 White Pyramids
- White Gemstones & Crystals for North-West:-
  - ➤ Clear Quartz
  - ➤ White Agate
  - ➤ Adra Stone^^
  - ➤ White Jade
  - ➤ Fully Round Natural Pearl^
  - ➤ Mother of Pearl
  - ➤ Moonstone
  - ➤ Triphane Gemstone^^
- Directional Healing Crystal for North-West
- Secret Programmed Vastu Diviner^^ for North-West
- Negativity Cleaning Crystals
- Salt Lamp
- Megha Mani^^
- Rudraksha for North-West:-
  - ➤ 4 Mukhi Rudraksha
  - ➤ 13 Mukhi Rudraksha
  - ➤ 22 Mukhi Rudraksha^
  - ➤ 1 Mukhi Trinetra Rudraksha^^
  - ➤ 1 Mukhi Jyotir Lingum Rudraksha^^
- Moon Rock^
- Aakash Mani Nubh Mani^^
- Infinity Gem^^ (Faco Crystal) White
- Pearl White Color
- Protection Bug Fossil^^^
- Narmadeshwar Shivling White
- Pearl Blisters
- Bidaal Mani^^^
- Siyar Singhi Joda Male Female Pair

Remedies for Reduction / Cutout in North:-

- Pure Stone Pyramid
- 3 or 6 Green Pyramids
- Gemstones & Crystals for North:-
  - Green Jade
  - Conk Stone^^^
  - Green Aventurine
  - Green Agate
  - Green Garnet
  - Green Tourmaline
  - Peridot
  - Hiddenite^
  - Green Amber
  - Green Turquoise
  - Malachite
  - Oyester Pearl^^
  - Moti Mani^^
  - Green Fluorite
  - Green Jasper
  - Amazonite
  - Florite
  - Samudrik Stone^^
  - Parasha Gemstone^^^
  - Green Tourmaline
  - Green Beryl^
- Green Water Pyramid
- Directional Healing Crystal for North
- Secret Programmed Vastu Diviner^^ for North
- Specially Formulated Vastu Dosh Nivaran Yantra*^ for North
- Water Charging Crystals
- Negativity Cleaning Crystals
- Salt Lamp
- Rudraksha for North:-
  - 3 Mukhi Rudraksha
  - 6 Mukhi Rudraksha
  - 15 Mukhi Rudraksha

- ➢ 21 Mukhi Rudraksha^
- ➢ 25 Mukhi Rudraksha^^
- ➢ 30 Mukhi Rudraksha^^
- Money Eggs^^
- Infinity Gem^^ (Faco Crystal) Green
- Morogul Mani^
- Green Color
- Plants
- Samudrik Mani^^
- Raw Emerald
- Conk Pearl Gilabi Mani^^^
- Indrajaal, Brahmajaal
- Jungli Kaali Billi ki Jer*^^
- Hatha Jodi with Actual Root
- Saam Siyar Singhi
- Sahastra Sampudh Mani^
- Dakshinavarti Shankh
- Dhan ka Bandha*^
- Asphetic Shri Yantra

Remedies for Roads Around

In this section, we have provided the right vastu correction tools and vastu dosh nivaran products to be used to rectify ill effects of roads around the dwelling.

Remedies for Road in North-West:-

- Pure Stone Pyramid
- 4 White Pyramids
- Directional Healing Crystal for North-West
- Secret Programmed Vastu Diviner^^ for North-West
- Negativity Cleaning Crystals
- Salt Lamp
- Megha Mani^^
- Rudraksha for North-West:-
  - 4 Mukhi Rudraksha
  - 13 Mukhi Rudraksha
  - 22 Mukhi Rudraksha^
  - 1 Mukhi Trinetra Rudraksha^^
  - 1 Mukhi Jyotir Lingum Rudraksha^^

- Moon Rock^
- Aakash Mani Nubh Mani^^
- Infinity Gem^^ (Faco Crystal) White
- Pearl White Color
- Protection Bug Fossil^^^
- Narmadeshwar Shivling White
- Pearl Blisters
- Bidaal Mani^^^
- Siyar Singhi Joda Male Female Pair

Remedies for Road in West:-

- Pure Stone Pyramid
- 10 or 11 Black / Blue Pyramids
- Blue Water Pyramid
- Directional Healing Crystal for West
- Secret Programmed Vastu Diviner^^ for West
- Specially Formulated Vastu Dosh Nivaran Yantra*^ for West
- Water Charging Crystals
- Negativity Cleaning Crystals
- Salt Lamp
- Morogul Mani^
- Conk Pearl Gilabi Mani^^^
- Education Tower
- Rudraksha for West:-
  - 10 Mukhi Rudraksha
  - 11 Mukhi Rudraksha
  - 19 Mukhi Rudraksha
  - 28 Mukhi Rudraksha^^
  - 29 Mukhi Rudraksha^^
  - 1 Mukhi Trinetra Rudraksha^^
  - 1 Mukhi Jyotir Lingum Rudraksha^^
- Raw Sugilite Crystal
- Raw Turquoise Crystals

- Black & Blue Colors
- Infinity Gem^^ (Faco Crystal) Green
- Narmadeshwar Shivling Black
- Saam Siyar Singhi
- Jungli Kaali Billi ki Jer*^^
- Hatha Jodi
- Gaj Mukta^^^
- Dakshinavarti Shankh
- Sahastra Sampudh Mani^
- Dhan ka Bandha^
- Samudrik Mani^^

Remedies for Road in South-West:-

- Pure Stone Pyramid
- 10 or 11 Brown Pyramids
- Directional Healing Crystal for South-West
- Secret Programmed Vastu Diviner^^ for South-West
- Specially Formulated Vastu Dosh Nivaran Yantra*^ for South-West
- Negativity Cleaning Crystals
- Salt Lamp
- Rudrakshas for South-West:-
  - ➢ 10 Mukhi Rudraksha
  - ➢ 11 Mukhi Rudraksha
  - ➢ 19 Mukhi Rudraksha
  - ➢ 28 Mukhi Rudraksha^^
  - ➢ 29 Mukhi Rudraksha^^
  - ➢ 1 Mukhi Trinetra Rudraksha^^
  - ➢ 1 Mukhi Jyotir Lingum Rudraksha^^
  - ➢ Charam Pashupati Nath Rudraksha^^^
- Rahu ki Kaudi
- Venu Mani^^^
- Protection Bug Fossil^^^
- Brown & Grey Colors

- Naagmani Glowing^^
- Jungli Kaali Billi ki Jer*^^
- Hatha Jodi Jadh Samet (With Root)
- Brahmajaal
- Boar Pearl^^^
- Parad Shivling
- Shwetark Ganpati
- Talismani Mani for Enemies
- Sher ka Daant
- Shark Teeth
- Gaj Mukta^^^
- Antrikha / Space Stone / Space Stone Antrikha^^^

Remedies for Road in South:-

- Pure Stone Pyramid
- 8 Red Pyramids *
- Directional Healing Crystal for South
- Secret Programmed Vastu Diviner^^ for South
- Specially Formulated Vastu Dosh Nivaran Yantra*^ for South
- Negativity Cleaning Crystals
- Salt Lamp
- Rudrakshas for South:-
  - 1 Mukhi Rudraksha
  - 8 Mukhi Rudraksha
  - 17 Mukhi Rudraksha
  - 19 Mukhi Rudraksha^^
  - 26 Mukhi Rudraksha^^
  - 28 Mukhi Rudraksha^^
- Red Color
- Venu Mani^^^
- Raw Burmese Ruby
- Boar Pearl^^^
- Protection Bug Fossil^^^

- Red Lord Hanuman Photo / Idol
- Hatha Jodi Actual with Root
- Jungli Kaali Billi ki Jer*^^
- Kamakhaya Sindhoor
- Shwetark Ganpati
- Gaj Mukta^^^
- Jungli Suar ka Daant
- Dakshinavarti Shankh

Remedies for Road in South-East:-

- Pure Stone Pyramid
- 7 Grey Pyramids
- Directional Healing Crystal for South-East
- Secret Programmed Vastu Diviner*^^ for South-East
- Specially Formulated Vastu Dosh Nivaran Yantra*^ for South-East
- Deep Sea Corals *(Specific Patterns Needed)**
- Deep Sea Shells *(Specific Patterns Needed)**
- Pure & Natural Crystal Balls
- White Flowers
- Boar Pearl^^^
- Negativity Cleaning Crystals
- Salt Lamp
- Bidaal Mani^^^
- 925 Sterling Silver Artifacts
- Rudrakshas for South-East:-
  - 1 Mukhi Trinetra Rudraksha^^
  - 1 Mukhi Jyotir Lingum Rudraksha^^
  - 2 Mukhi Rudraksha
  - 7 Mukhi Rudraksha
  - 16 Mukhi Rudraksha
  - 20 Mukhi Rudraksha
  - 25 Mukhi Rudraksha^^

- Silver & Sparkling White Colors
- Infinity Gem^^ (Faco Crystal) White
- Kaama Siyar Singhi
- Protection Bug Fossil^^^
- Jungli Kaali Billi ki Jer*^^
- Kamakhaya Sindhoor

Remedies of Vidhisha / Vishudh Plot

In this section, we have provided the right vastu correction tools and vastu dosh nivaran products to be used to rectify ill effects of vidhisha or vishudh plots.

- Paasha Jaal^^^
- Protection Bug Fossil^^^
- Pure Stone Pyramid
- 9 or 12 Pyramids
- Yellow Water Pyramid
- Gems & Crystals:-
  - Jade
  - Aventurine
  - Jasper
  - Garnet
  - Conk Stone^^^
  - Citrine
  - Triphane Gemstone^^
  - Tourmaline
  - Topaz
  - Opal

- Oyester Pearl^^
  - Moti Mani^^
  - Labradorite
  - Agate
  - Florspar
  - Yellow Spodumene
  - Yellow Beryl
  - Scapolite
  - Samudrik Stone^^
  - Golden Yellow Japanese Coral
- Directional Healing Crystal for North-East
- Secret Programmed Vastu Diviner *^^ for North-East
- Specially Formulated Vastu Dosh Nivaran Yantra for North East *^
- Water Charging Crystals
- Negativity Cleaning Crystals
- Salt Lamp
- Rudrakshas for Vidisha or Vishudh Plot:-
  - 9 Mukhi Rudraksha
  - 12 Mukhi Rudraksha
  - 18 Mukhi Rudraksha
  - 27 Mukhi Rudraksha
- Indrajaal
- Morogul Mani^
- Conk Pearl Gilabi Mani^^^
- Yellow Color
- Protection Bug Fossil^^^
- Antrikha / Space Stone / Space Stone Antrikha*^^^
- Nav-Grah Pyramid Yantra
- Naagmani Glowing^^
- Kamakhya Sindhoor
- Sahastra Sampudh Mani^
- Parad Shivling
- Samudrik Mani^^

- Shwetark Ganpati
- Haldi ke Ganesh
- Kastoori

Remedies for Drainage & Septic Tank

In this section, we have provided the right vastu correction tools and vastu dosh nivaran products to be used to rectify ill effects of drainage and septic tanks in wrong directions.

Here are the remedies of Drainage & Septic Tank placed in the wrong Directions.

- Naagmani Black^^^
- Pure Stone Pyramid in North-East or Bhrahmasthan or South-West
- 9 or 12 Yellow Pyramids in North-East
- Gems & Crystals for Drainage & Septic Tank:-
  - Smokey Quartz
  - Bronzite
  - Agates
  - Grey Agates
  - Qabana Stonc^^
  - Tiger's Eye Crystal
  - Amber
  - Wolk Stone^^

- ➤ Smokey Topaz
- ➤ Hessonite Garnet
- ➤ Grey Japanese Coral
  - ➤ Scapolite
- ➤ Golden Yellow Japanese Coral
- Secret Programmed Vastu Diviner^^ for South-West & North East
- Specially Formulated Vastu Dosh Nivaran Yantra*^ for South-West & North East
- Rudrakshas for North-East: -
  - ➤ 9 Mukhi Rudraksha
  - ➤ 12 Mukhi Rudraksha
  - ➤ 18 Mukhi Rudraksha
- Rudraksha for Bhrahmasthan: -
  - ➤ 1 Mukhi Rudraksha Gole Dana
  - ➤ 21 Mukhi Rudraksha
  - ➤ Combination of 16 Mukhi Rudraksha + 17 Mukhi Rudraksha + 18 Mukhi Rudraksha
  - ➤ 1 Mukhi Java Rudraksha^^
  - ➤ 1 Mukhi Java Rudraksha Gehuaan Dana^^
  - ➤ Charam Pashupati Nath Rudraksha
- Protection Bug Fossil^^^
- Antrikha / Space Stone Antrikha *^
- Combination of Brahmajaal + Indrajaal
- Combination of Kaali Billi ki Jer + Siyar Singhi + Mota Hatha Jodi
- Combination of 20-140 Vastu Healing Products
- Asphetic Shri Yantra
- Protection Bug Fossil^^^
- Rahu ki Kaudi in South-West
- Kaali Billi ki Jer^^
- Hatha Jodi Jadh Samet (With Root)
- Brahmajaal
- Sher ka Daant
- Shark Teeth

Remedies for Water Tank, Overhead Water Tank

In this section, we have provided the right vastu correction tools and vastu dosh nivaran products to be used to rectify ill effects of water tanks, overhead water tanks in wrong directions.

- Paasha Jaal^^^
- Eagle Stone^^
- Adra Stone^^
- Fully Round Natural Pearl^
- White Triphane Gemstone^^

- Secret Programmed Vastu Diviner^^ for North-West & North East
- Megha Mani^^
- Moon Rock^
- Aakash Mani Nubh Mani^^
- Pearl Blisters
- Siyar Singhi Joda Male Female Pair
- Deep Sea Corals
- Deep Sea Shells
- White Flowers
- Rudraksha for North-West:-
  - 4 Mukhi Rudraksha
  - 13 Mukhi Rudraksha
  - 22 Mukhi Rudraksha^
  - 1 Mukhi Trinetra Rudraksha^^
  - 1 Mukhi Jyotir Lingum Rudraksha^^
  - 1 Mukhi Rudraksha Gole Dana
  - 1 Mukhi Java Rudraksha^^
  - 1 Mukhi Java Rudraksha Gehuaan Dana^^
  - 21 Mukhi Rudraksha
  - Combination of 16 Mukhi Rudraksha + 17 Mukhi Rudraksha + 18 Mukhi Rudraksha
  - Charam Pashupati Nath Rudraksha

Remedies for Underground Water Tank

In this section, we have provided the right vastu correction tools and vastu dosh nivaran products to be used to rectify ill effects of underground water tanks in wrong directions.

Remedies for Underground Water Tank in North-West are:-

- Paaras Booti^^^
- Timi Stone^^^
- Pure Stone Pyramid
- 4 White Pyramids
- White Gemstones & Crystals:-
  - ➢ Clear Quartz
  - ➢ White Agate
  - ➢ White Jade
  - ➢ Natural Pearl
  - ➢ Mother of Pearl
  - ➢ Moonstone
- Secret Programmed Vastu Diviner^^ for North-West
- Megha Mani^^
- Moon Rock^
- Aakash Mani Nubh Mani^^
- Narmadeshwar Shivling White
- Pearl Blisters
- Bidaal Mani^^^

Remedies of Underground Water Tank in West:-

- Secret Programmed Vastu Diviner^^ for West
- Specially Formulated Vastu Dosh Nivaran Yantra*^ for West

39

- Gemstones & Crystals:-
  - ➤ Lapis Lazuli
  - ➤ Hematite
  - ➤ Angelite
  - ➤ Oyester Pearl^^
  - ➤ Moti Mani^^
  - ➤ Black Obsidian
  - ➤ Blue Tourmaline
  - ➤ Aquamarine
  - ➤ Blue Agate
  - ➤ Black Agate
  - ➤ Iolite
  - ➤ Conk Stone^^^
  - ➤ Sodalite
  - ➤ Blue Fluorite
  - ➤ Blue Amber
  - ➤ Azurite
  - ➤ Black Opal
  - ➤ Black Pearl
  - ➤ Black Onyx
  - ➤ Black Tourmaline
  - ➤ Kyanite
  - ➤ Cordierite
  - ➤ Samudrik Stone^^
  - ➤ Purple Sapphire
  - ➤ Japanese Blue Coral
  - ➤ Japanese Black Coral
  - ➤ Black Spinel
- Paaras Booti^^^
- Timi Stone^^^
- Water Charging Crystals
- Negativity Cleaning Crystals
- Morogul Mani^
- Conk Pearl Gilabi Mani^^^
- Raw Sugilite Crystal
- Raw Turquoise Crystals
- Narmadeshwar Shivling Black

- Gaj Mukta^^^
- Dakshinavarti Shankh
- Sahastra Sampudh Mani^
- Dhan ka Bandha^
- Samudrik Mani^^

Remedies of Underground Water Tank in South-West:-

- Paaras Booti^^^
- Timi Stone^^^
- Venu Mani^^^
- Naagmani Glowing^^
- Boar Pearl^^^
- Gemstones & Crystals:-
  - Smokey Quartz
  - Bronzite
  - Brown Agates
  - Grey Agates
  - Qabana Stone^^
  - Tiger's Eye Crystal
  - Amber
  - Wolk Stone^^
  - Smokey Topaz
  - Hessonite Garnet
  - Grey Japanese Coral
- Protection Bug Fossil^^^
- Antrikha / Space Stone / Space Stone Antrikha^^^
- Secret Programmed Vastu Diviner^^ for South-West
- Specially Formulated Vastu Dosh Nivaran Yantra*^ for South-West
- Rahu ki Kaudi
- Parad Shivling
- Shwetark Ganpati
- Sher ka Daant

- Shark Teeth
- Gaj Mukta^^^

Remedies of Underground Water Tank in South:-

- Raw Burmese Ruby
- Boar Pearl^^^
- Paaras Booti^^^
- Timi Stone^^^
- Red Gemstones & Crystals:-
  - Carnelian
  - Red Garnet
  - Qabana Stone^^
  - Red Jasper
  - Red Agate
  - Red Fluorite
  - Wolk Stone^^
  - Red Sapphire
  - Red Spinel
  - Red Coral
  - Heart Shaped Coral
- Secret Programmed Vastu Diviner^^ for South
- Specially Formulated Vastu Dosh Nivaran Yantra*^ for South
- Venu Mani^^^
- Shwetark Ganpati
- Gaj Mukta^^^
- Protection Bug Fossil^^^
- Jungli Suar ka Daant
- Dakshinavarti Shankh

Remedies of Toilet, Bathroom & Attached Toilet-Bathroom

In this section, we have provided the right vastu correction tools and vastu dosh nivaran products to be used to rectify ill effects of toilets, bathrooms and attached toilet bathrooms in wrong directions.

Remedies of Toilet, Bathroom & Attached Toilet-Bathroom in North-East

- Secret Programmed Vastu Diviner *^^ for North-East
- Specially Formulated Vastu Dosh Nivaran Yantra for North East *^
- 9 or 12 Yellow Pyramids
- Yellow Water Pyramid
- Water Charging Crystals
- Negativity Cleaning Crystals
- Salt Lamp

- Indrajaal
- Morogul Mani^
- Conk Pearl Gilabi Mani^^^
- Yellow Color
- Protection Bug Fossil^^^
- Antrikha / Space Stone / Space Stone Antrikha*^^^
- Nav-Grah Pyramid Yantra
- Naagmani Glowing^^
- Sahastra Sampudh Mani^
- Parad Shivling
- Samudrik Mani^^
- Kastoori
- Gems & Crystals:-
  - Yellow Jade
  - Yellow Aventurine
  - Yellow Jasper
  - Yellow Garnet
  - Conk Stone^^^
  - Deep Yellow Citrine
  - Yellow Triphane Gemstone^^
  - Yellow Tourmaline
  - Yellow Topaz
  - Yellow Opal
  - Oyester Pearl^^
  - Moti Mani^^
  - Yellow Labradorite
  - Yellow Agate
  - Yellow Florspar
  - Yellow Spodumene
  - Yellow Beryl
  - Scapolite
  - Samudrik Stone^^
  - Golden Yellow Japanese Coral
- Rudrakshas:-
  - 9 Mukhi Rudraksha

- ➢ 12 Mukhi Rudraksha
- ➢ 18 Mukhi Rudraksha
- ➢ 27 Mukhi Rudraksha

Remedies of Toilet, Bathroom& Attached Toilet-Bathroom in East

- Orange Color
- Infinity Gem^^ (Faco Crystal) Green
- Sher Ka Daant (Lions Teeth)
- Junglee Suar ka Daant (Wild Pig Teeth)
- Directional Healing Crystal for East
- Secret Programmed Vastu Diviner^^ for East
- Specially Formulated Vastu Dosh Nivaran Yantra*^ for East
- Morogul Mani^
- Sahastra Sampudh Mani^
- Water Charging Crystals
- Negativity Cleaning Crystals
- Pure Stone Pyramid
- 5 Orange Pyramids
- Orange Water Pyramid
- Salt Lamp
- Conk Pearl Gilabi Mani^^^
- Gems & Crystals:-
  - ➢ Orange Sunstone
  - ➢ Orange Topaz
  - ➢ Orange Tourmaline
  - ➢ Orange Garnet
  - ➢ Orange Opal
  - ➢ Conk Stone^^^
  - ➢ Orange Sphalerite
  - ➢ Orange Flourite
  - ➢ Carnelian
  - ➢ Oyester Pearl^^
  - ➢ Moti Mani^^
  - ➢ Orange Agate

- ➢ Peach Aventurine
- ➢ Orange Beryl
- ➢ Orange Citrine
- ➢ Samudrik Stone^^
- ➢ Amber
- Rudrakshas:-
  - ➢ 5 Mukhi Rudraksha
  - ➢ 14 Mukhi Rudraksha
  - ➢ 23 Mukhi Rudraksha

Remedies of Toilet, Bathroom & Attached Toilet-Bathroom in South-East

- Directional Healing Crystal for South-East
- Secret Programmed Vastu Diviner*^^ for South-East
- Specially Formulated Vastu Dosh Nivaran Yantra*^ for South-East
- Deep Sea Corals *(Specific Patterns Needed)*
- Deep Sea Shells *(Specific Patterns Needed)*
- Pure Stone Pyramid
- 7 Silver Pyramids
- Protection Bug Fossil^^^
- Pure & Natural Crystal Balls
- White Flowers
- Boar Pearl^^^
- Negativity Cleaning Crystals
- Salt Lamp
- Bidaal Mani^^^
- Silver & Sparkling White Colors
- Kaama Siyar Singhi
- Jungli Kaali Billi ki Jer*^^
- Kamakhaya Sindhoor
- 925 Sterling Silver Artifacts
- Gemstones & Crystals:-
  - ➢ Cubic Zirconia

- ➢ Zircon
- ➢ Asphetic
- ➢ Qabana Stone^^
- ➢ White Topaz
- ➢ White Spodumene
- ➢ Opal
- ➢ Triphane Gemstone^^
- ➢ White Beryl
- Rudrakshas:-
  - ➢ 1 Mukhi Trinetra Rudraksha^^
  - ➢ 1 Mukhi Jyotir Lingum Rudraksha^^
  - ➢ 2 Mukhi Rudraksha
  - ➢ 7 Mukhi Rudraksha
  - ➢ 16 Mukhi Rudraksha
  - ➢ 20 Mukhi Rudraksha
  - ➢ 25 Mukhi Rudraksha^^

Remedies of Toilet, Bathroom& Attached Toilet-Bathroom in West

- Pure Stone Pyramid
- 10 or 11 Black / Blue Pyramids
- Narmadeshwar Shivling Black
- Saam Siyar Singhi
- Jungli Kaali Billi ki Jer*^^
- Blue Water Pyramid
- Directional Healing Crystal for West
- Secret Programmed Vastu Diviner^^ for West
- Specially Formulated Vastu Dosh Nivaran Yantra*^ for West
- Water Charging Crystals
- Negativity Cleaning Crystals
- Salt Lamp
- Morogul Mani^
- Conk Pearl Gilabi Mani^^^
- Hatha Jodi
- Gaj Mukta^^^

- Dakshinavarti Shankh
- Sahastra Sampudh Mani^
- Dhan ka Bandha^
- Samudrik Mani^^
- Raw Sugilite Crystal
- Raw Turquoise Crystals
- Black & Blue Colors
- Gemstones & Crystals:-
  - Lapis Lazuli
  - Hematite
  - Angelite
  - Oyester Pearl^^
  - Moti Mani^^
  - Black Obsidian
  - Blue Tourmaline
  - Aquamarine
  - Blue Agate
  - Black Agate
  - Iolite
  - Conk Stone^^^
  - Sodalite
  - Blue Fluorite
  - Blue Amber
  - Azurite
  - Black Opal
  - Black Pearl
  - Black Onyx
  - Black Tourmaline
  - Kyanite
  - Cordierite
  - Samudrik Stone^^
  - Purple Sapphire
  - Japanese Blue Coral
  - Japanese Black Coral
  - Black Spinel
- Rudraksha:-
  - 10 Mukhi Rudraksha

- ➢ 11 Mukhi Rudraksha
- ➢ 19 Mukhi Rudraksha
- ➢ 28 Mukhi Rudraksha^^
- ➢ 29 Mukhi Rudraksha^^
- ➢ 1 Mukhi Trinetra Rudraksha^^
- ➢ 1 Mukhi Jyotir Lingum Rudraksha^^

Remedies of Toilet, Bathroom& Attached Toilet-Bathroom in North

- Morogul Mani^
- Green Color
- Plants
- Samudrik Mani^^
- Raw Emerald
- Conk Pearl Gilabi Mani^^^
- Indrajaal, Brahmajaal
- Jungli Kaali Billi ki Jer*^^
- Hatha Jodi with Actual Root
- Sahastra Sampudh Mani^
- Dakshinavarti Shankh
- Asphetic Shri Yantra
- Pure Stone Pyramid
- 3 or 6 Green Pyramids
- Green Water Pyramid
- Directional Healing Crystal for North
- Secret Programmed Vastu Diviner^^ for North
- Specially Formulated Vastu Dosh Nivaran Yantra*^ for North
- Water Charging Crystals
- Negativity Cleaning Crystals
- Salt Lamp
- Gemstones & Crystals:-
  - ➢ Green Jade
  - ➢ Conk Stone^^^

- ➤ Green Aventurine
- ➤ Green Agate
- ➤ Green Garnet
- ➤ Green Tourmaline
- ➤ Peridot
- ➤ Hiddenite^
- ➤ Green Amber
- ➤ Green Turquoise
- ➤ Malachite
- ➤ Oyester Pearl^^
- ➤ Moti Mani^^
- ➤ Green Fluorite
- ➤ Green Jasper
- ➤ Amazonite
- ➤ Florite
- ➤ Samudrik Stone^^
- ➤ Parasha Gemstone^^^
- ➤ Green Tourmaline
- ➤ Green Beryl^
- Rudraksha:-
  - ➤ 3 Mukhi Rudraksha
  - ➤ 6 Mukhi Rudraksha
  - ➤ 15 Mukhi Rudraksha
  - ➤ 21 Mukhi Rudraksha^
  - ➤ 25 Mukhi Rudraksha^^
  - ➤ 30 Mukhi Rudraksha^^

Remedies of Toilet, Bathroom& Attached Toilet-Bathroom in Bhrahmasthan

- Kale Ghodhe ki Naal^
- Antrikha / Space Stone / Space Stone Antrikha^^^
- Vishnu Chakra Moti^^
- Fully Round Natural Pearl^
- Tutmak Stone^^
- Protection Bug Fossil^^^
- Naagmani Glowing^^^

- Protection Bug Fossil^^^
- c
- Combination of Kaali Billi ki Jer + Siyar Singhi + Mota Hatha Jodi
- Kamakhaya Sindoor
- Parad Shivling
- Combination of 20-140 Vastu Healing Products
- Kastoori
- Asphetic Shri Yantra
- Timi Stone^^
- Adra Stone^^
- Water Charging Crystals
- Negativity Cleaning Crystals
- Salt Lamp
- **Conk Stone^^^**
- Qabana Stone^^
- Protection Bug Fossil^^^
- Eagle Stone^^^
- White Triphane Gemstone ^^
- Nav-Grah Pyramid Yantra
- Gemstones & Crystals for South-East:-
  - ➢ Cubic Zirconia
  - ➢ Zircon
  - ➢ Asphetic
  - ➢ Qabana Stone^^
  - ➢ White Topaz
  - ➢ White Spodumene
  - ➢ Opal
  - ➢ Triphane Gemstone^^
  - ➢ White Beryl
- Rudraksha for Bhrahmasthan:-
  - ➢ 1 Mukhi Rudraksha Gole Dana
  - ➢ 21 Mukhi Rudraksha
  - ➢ Combination of 16 Mukhi Rudraksha + 17 Mukhi Rudraksha + 18 Mukhi Rudraksha
  - ➢ 1 Mukhi Java Rudraksha^^

- 1 Mukhi Java Rudraksha Gehuaan Dana^^
- Charam Pashupati Nath Rudraksha

Remedies of Kitchen

In this section, we have provided the right vastu correction tools and vastu dosh nivaran products to be used to rectify ill effects of Kitchen in wrong directions.

Remedies of Kitchen in North-East

- 9 or 12 Yellow Pyramids
- 7 Silver Pyramids
- Secret Programmed Vastu Diviner*^^ for South-East
- Specially Formulated Vastu Dosh Nivaran Yantra*^ for South-East
- Deep Sea Corals *(Specific Patterns Needed)*
- Deep Sea Shells *(Specific Patterns Needed)*
- White Flowers
- Boar Pearl^^^
- Bidaal Mani^^^
- Kaama Siyar Singhi
- Jungli Kaali Billi ki Jer*^^

- Kamakhaya Sindhoor
- Protection Bug Fossil^^^
- Directional Healing Crystal for North-East
- Secret Programmed Vastu Diviner *^^ for North-East
- Specially Formulated Vastu Dosh Nivaran Yantra for North East *^
- Indrajaal
- Morogul Mani^
- Conk Pearl Gilabi Mani^^^
- Antrikha / Space Stone / Space Stone Antrikha*^^^
- Nav-Grah Pyramid Yantra
- Naagmani Glowing^^
- Kamakhya Sindhoor
- Sahastra Sampudh Mani^
- Parad Shivling
- Samudrik Mani^^
- Shwetark Ganpati
- Haldi ke Ganesh
- Kastoori
- Gems & Crystals:-
  - Yellow Jade
  - Yellow Aventurine
  - Yellow Jasper
  - Yellow Garnet
  - Conk Stone^^^
  - Deep Yellow Citrine
  - Yellow Triphane Gemstone^^
  - Yellow Tourmaline
  - Yellow Topaz
  - Yellow Opal
  - Oyester Pearl^^
  - Moti Mani^^
  - Yellow Labradorite
  - Yellow Agate

- ➢ Yellow Florspar
- ➢ Yellow Spodumene
- ➢ Yellow Beryl
- ➢ Scapolite
- ➢ Samudrik Stone^^
- ➢ Golden Yellow Japanese Coral
- ➢ Cubic Zirconia
- ➢ Zircon
- ➢ Asphetic
- ➢ Qabana Stone^^
- ➢ White Topaz
- ➢ White Spodumene
- ➢ Opal
- ➢ Triphane Gemstone^^
- ➢ White Beryl

Remedies of Kitchen in East

- 7 Silver Pyramids
- 5 Orange Pyramids
- Secret Programmed Vastu Diviner*^^ for South-East
- Specially Formulated Vastu Dosh Nivaran Yantra*^ for South-East
- Deep Sea Corals (Specific Patterns Needed)*
- Deep Sea Shells (Specific Patterns Needed)*
- Secret Programmed Vastu Diviner^^ for East
- Specially Formulated Vastu Dosh Nivaran Yantra*^ for East
- Morogul Mani^
- Sahastra Sampudh Mani^
- Conk Pearl Gilabi Mani^^^
- Sher Ka Daant (Lions Teeth)
- Junglee Suar ka Daant (Wild Pig Teeth)
- White Flowers
- Boar Pearl^^^
- Bidaal Mani^^^

- Kaama Siyar Singhi
- Jungli Kaali Billi ki Jer*^^
- Kamakhaya Sindhoor
- Gems & Crystals:-
  - Orange Sunstone
  - Orange Topaz
  - Orange Tourmaline
  - Orange Garnet
  - Orange Opal
  - Conk Stone^^^
  - Orange Sphalerite
  - Orange Flourite
  - Carnelian
  - Oyester Pearl^^
  - Moti Mani^^
  - Orange Agate
  - Peach Aventurine
  - Orange Beryl
  - Orange Citrine
  - Samudrik Stone^^
  - Cubic Zirconia
  - Zircon
  - Asphetic
  - Qabana Stone^^
  - White Topaz
  - White Spodumene
  - Opal
  - Triphane Gemstone^^
  - White Beryl
  - Amber

Remedies of Kitchen in South

- 8 Red Pyramids *
- 7 Silver Pyramids
- Secret Programmed Vastu Diviner*^^ for South-East

- Specially Formulated Vastu Dosh Nivaran Yantra*^ for South-East
- Deep Sea Corals *(Specific Patterns Needed)**
- Deep Sea Shells *(Specific Patterns Needed)**
- Pure Stone Pyramid
- White Flowers
- Boar Pearl^^^
- Bidaal Mani^^^
- Kaama Siyar Singhi
- Protection Bug Fossil^^^
- Secret Programmed Vastu Diviner^^ for South
- Specially Formulated Vastu Dosh Nivaran Yantra*^ for South
- Negativity Cleaning Crystals
- Venu Mani^^^
- Raw Burmese Ruby
- Boar Pearl^^^
- Red Lord Hanuman Photo / Idol
- Hatha Jodi Actual with Root
- Jungli Kaali Billi ki Jer*^^
- Kamakhaya Sindhoor
- Shwetark Ganpati
- Gaj Mukta^^^
- Jungli Suar ka Daant
- Dakshinavarti Shankh
- Gemstones & Crystals:-
  - ➢ Carnelian
  - ➢ Red Garnet
  - ➢ Qabana Stone^^
  - ➢ Red Jasper
  - ➢ Red Agate
  - ➢ Red Fluorite
  - ➢ Wolk Stone^^
  - ➢ Red Sapphire
  - ➢ Red Spinel

- Red Coral
- Cubic Zirconia
- Zircon
- Asphetic
- Qabana Stone^^
- White Topaz
- White Spodumene
- Opal
- Triphane Gemstone^^
- White Beryl
- Heart Shaped Coral

Remedies of Kitchen in West

- 10 or 11 Black / Blue Pyramids
- 7 Silver Pyramids
- Secret Programmed Vastu Diviner*^^ for South-East
- Specially Formulated Vastu Dosh Nivaran Yantra*^ for South-East
- Secret Programmed Vastu Diviner^^ for West
- Specially Formulated Vastu Dosh Nivaran Yantra*^ for West
- Deep Sea Corals *(Specific Patterns Needed)*
- Deep Sea Shells *(Specific Patterns Needed)*
- White Flowers
- Boar Pearl^^^
- Bidaal Mani^^^
- Kaama Siyar Singhi
- Jungli Kaali Billi ki Jer*^^
- Hatha Jodi
- Gaj Mukta^^^
- Kamakhaya Sindhoor
- Pure Stone Pyramid
- Morogul Mani^
- Raw Sugilite Crystal

- Raw Turquoise Crystals
- Narmadeshwar Shivling Black
- Saam Siyar Singhi
- Jungli Kaali Billi ki Jer*^^
- Dakshinavarti Shankh
- Sahastra Sampudh Mani^
- Dhan ka Bandha^
- Samudrik Mani^^
- Conk Pearl Gilabi Mani^^^
- Gemstones & Crystals for West:-
  - Lapis Lazuli
  - Hematite
  - Angelite
  - Oyester Pearl^^
  - Moti Mani^^
  - Black Obsidian
  - Blue Tourmaline
  - Aquamarine
  - Blue Agate
  - Black Agate
  - Iolite
  - Conk Stone^^^
  - Sodalite
  - Blue Fluorite
  - Blue Amber
  - Azurite
  - Black Opal
  - Black Pearl
  - Black Onyx
  - Black Tourmaline
  - Kyanite
  - Cordierite
  - Purple Sapphire
  - Japanese Blue Coral
  - Japanese Black Coral
  - Black Spinel
  - Cubic Zirconia

- ➤ Zircon
- ➤ Asphetic
- ➤ Qabana Stone^^
- ➤ White Topaz
- ➤ White Spodumene
- ➤ Opal
- ➤ Triphane Gemstone^^
- ➤ White Beryl
- ➤ Samudrik Stone^^
- Rudraksha:-
  - ➤ 10 Mukhi Rudraksha
  - ➤ 2 Mukhi Rudraksha
  - ➤ 7 Mukhi Rudraksha
  - ➤ 16 Mukhi Rudraksha
  - ➤ 20 Mukhi Rudraksha
  - ➤ 25 Mukhi Rudraksha^^
  - ➤ 11 Mukhi Rudraksha
  - ➤ 19 Mukhi Rudraksha
  - ➤ 28 Mukhi Rudraksha^^
  - ➤ 29 Mukhi Rudraksha^^
  - ➤ 1 Mukhi Trinetra Rudraksha^^
  - ➤ 1 Mukhi Jyotir Lingum Rudraksha^^

Remedies of Kitchen in North-West

- Secret Programmed Vastu Diviner*^^ for South-East
- Specially Formulated Vastu Dosh Nivaran Yantra*^ for South-East
- Directional Healing Crystal for North-West
- Secret Programmed Vastu Diviner^^ for North-West
- Deep Sea Corals (*Specific Patterns Needed*)*
- Deep Sea Shells (*Specific Patterns Needed*)*
- Protection Bug Fossil^^^
- Pure & Natural Crystal Balls
- White Flowers

- Boar Pearl^^^
- Bidaal Mani^^^
- Kaama Siyar Singhi
- Jungli Kaali Billi ki Jer*^^
- Kamakhaya Sindhoor
- Pure Stone Pyramid
- 7 Silver Pyramids
- 4 White Pyramids
- Megha Mani^^
- Moon Rock^
- Aakash Mani Nubh Mani^^
- Narmadeshwar Shivling White
- Pearl Blisters
- Bidaal Mani^^^
- Siyar Singhi Joda Male Female Pair
- Gemstones & Crystals:-
  - Clear Quartz
  - White Agate
  - Adra Stone^^
  - White Jade
  - Fully Round Natural Pearl^
  - Mother of Pearl
  - Moonstone
  - Triphane Gemstone^^
  - Cubic Zirconia
  - Zircon
  - Asphetic
  - Qabana Stone^^
  - White Topaz
  - White Spodumene
  - Opal
  - Triphane Gemstone^^
  - White Beryl
  - 25 Mukhi Rudraksha^^

Remedies of Kitchen in North

- Secret Programmed Vastu Diviner*^^ for South-East
- Specially Formulated Vastu Dosh Nivaran Yantra*^ for South-East
- Secret Programmed Vastu Diviner^^ for North
- Specially Formulated Vastu Dosh Nivaran Yantra*^ for North
- Deep Sea Corals (*Specific Patterns Needed*)*
- Deep Sea Shells (*Specific Patterns Needed*)*
- Pure Stone Pyramid
- 3 or 6 Green Pyramids
- 7 Silver Pyramids
- White Flowers
- Boar Pearl^^^
- Bidaal Mani^^^
- Jungli Kaali Billi ki Jer*^^
- Kamakhaya Sindhoor
- Morogul Mani^
- Plants
- Samudrik Mani^^
- Raw Emerald
- Conk Pearl Gilabi Mani^^^
- Indrajaal, Brahmajaal
- Jungli Kaali Billi ki Jer*^^
- Hatha Jodi with Actual Root
- Saam Siyar Singhi
- Sahastra Sampudh Mani^
- Dakshinavarti Shankh
- Dhan ka Bandha*^
- Asphetic Shri Yantra
- Gemstones & Crystals:-
  - Cubic Zirconia
  - Zircon
  - Asphetic

- ➢ Qabana Stone^^
- ➢ White Topaz
- ➢ White Spodumene
- ➢ Opal
- ➢ Green Jade
- ➢ Conk Stone^^^
- ➢ Green Aventurine
- ➢ Green Agate
- ➢ Green Garnet
- ➢ Green Tourmaline
- ➢ Peridot
- ➢ Hiddenite^
- ➢ Green Amber
- ➢ Green Turquoise
- ➢ Malachite
- ➢ Oyester Pearl^^
- ➢ Moti Mani^^
- ➢ Green Fluorite
- ➢ Green Jasper
- ➢ Amazonite
- ➢ Florite
- ➢ Samudrik Stone^^
- ➢ Parasha Gemstone^^^
- ➢ Green Tourmaline
- ➢ Green Beryl^
- ➢ Triphane Gemstone^^
- ➢ White Beryl
- • Rudrakshas:-
  - ➢ 1 Mukhi Trinetra Rudraksha^^
  - ➢ 1 Mukhi Jyotir Lingum Rudraksha^^
  - ➢ 2 Mukhi Rudraksha
  - ➢ 7 Mukhi Rudraksha
  - ➢ 16 Mukhi Rudraksha
  - ➢ 20 Mukhi Rudraksha
  - ➢ 25 Mukhi Rudraksha^^
  - ➢ 3 Mukhi Rudraksha
  - ➢ 6 Mukhi Rudraksha

> 15 Mukhi Rudraksha
> 21 Mukhi Rudraksha^
> 25 Mukhi Rudraksha^^
> 30 Mukhi Rudraksha^^

Remedies of Kitchen in Brahmasthaan

- Secret Programmed Vastu Diviner^^ for Brahmasthaan
- Specially Formulated Vastu Dosh Nivaran Yantra^^ for Brahmasthaan
- Kale Ghodhe ki Naal
- Antrikha / Space Stone / Space Stone Antrikha^^^
- Infinity Gem^^ (Faco Crystal) White & Green
- Vishnu Chakra Moti^^
- Fully Round Natural Pearl^^
- Tutmak Stone^^
- Timi Stone^^^
- Adra Stone^^
- Enemy Stone^^
- **Conk Stone^^^**
- Qabana Stone^^^
- Protection Bug Fossil^^^
- Eagle Stone^^^
- Triphane Gemstone ^^
- Cordierite^^
- Nagmani Black^
- Naagmani Glowing^^^
- Jungli Kaali Billi ki Jer
- Parad Shivling
- Deep Sea Corals^
- Deep Sea Shells^
- Combination of 120-140 Vastu Healing Products
- Moon Rock^^
- Natural Pearl Blisters

- Rudraksha:-
  - 1 Mukhi Rudraksha Gole Dana
  - 21 Mukhi Rudraksha
  - Combination of 16 Mukhi Rudraksha + 17 Mukhi Rudraksha + 18 Mukhi Rudraksha
  - Charam Pashupati Nath Rudraksha
  - 1 Mukhi Java Rudraksha^^
  - 1 Mukhi Java Rudraksha Gehuaan Dana^^
- Gemstones: Hiddenite, Parasha, Green Beryl, Green Florite, Yellow Florspar, Yellow Beryl, Yellow Spodumene

Remedies of Kitchen in South West

- Secret Programmed Vastu Diviner^^ for South-West
- Specially Formulated Vastu Dosh Nivaran Yantra*^ for South-West
- Rahu ki Kaudi
- Venu Mani^^^
- Naagmani Glowing^^
- Jungli Kaali Billi ki Jer*^^
- Hatha Jodi Jadh Samet (With Root)
- Protection Bug Fossil^^^
- Boar Pearl^^^
- Antrikha / Space Stone / Space Stone Antrikha^^^
- Gaj Mukta^^^
- Gemstones & Crystals:-
  - Qabana Stone^^
  - Wolk Stone^^
  - Grey Japanese Coral
- Rudrakshas:-
  - 19 Mukhi Rudraksha
  - 28 Mukhi Rudraksha^^
  - 29 Mukhi Rudraksha^^
  - 1 Mukhi Trinetra Rudraksha^^

➢ 1 Mukhi Jyotir Lingum Rudraksha^^
➢ Charam Pashupati Nath Rudraksha^^^

Remedies of Mandir / Prayer Room / Puja Room / Temple at Home

In this section, we have provided the right vastu correction tools and vastu dosh nivaran products to be used to rectify ill effects of mandir, prayer room, puja room, temple at home in wrong directions.

Remedies of Mandir / Prayer Room / Puja Room in East

- Directional Healing Crystal for East
- Secret Programmed Vastu Diviner^^ for East
- Specially Formulated Vastu Dosh Nivaran Yantra*^ for East

- Morogul Mani^
- Sahastra Sampudh Mani^
- Water Charging Crystals
- Negativity Cleaning Crystals
- Salt Lamp
- Conk Pearl Gilabi Mani^^^
- Orange Color
- Infinity Gem^^ (Faco Crystal) Green
- Sher Ka Daant (Lions Teeth)
- Junglee Suar ka Daant (Wild Pig Teeth)
- Pure Stone Pyramid
- 5 Orange Pyramids
- Orange Water Pyramid
- Gems & Crystals:-
  - Orange Sunstone
  - Orange Topaz
  - Orange Tourmaline
  - Orange Garnet
  - Orange Opal
  - Conk Stone^^^
  - Orange Sphalerite
  - Orange Flourite
  - Carnelian
  - Oyester Pearl^^
  - Moti Mani^^
  - Orange Agate
  - Peach Aventurine
  - Orange Beryl
  - Orange Citrine
  - Samudrik Stone^^
  - Amber
- Rudrakshas:-
  - 14 Mukhi Rudraksha
  - 23 Mukhi Rudraksha

Remedies of Mandir / Prayer Room / Puja Room in South-East

- Gemstones & Crystals:-
  - Cubic Zirconia
  - Zircon
  - Asphetic
  - Qabana Stone^^
  - White Topaz
  - White Spodumene
  - Opal
  - Triphane Gemstone^^
  - White Beryl
- Directional Healing Crystal for South-East
- Secret Programmed Vastu Diviner*^^ for South-East
- Specially Formulated Vastu Dosh Nivaran Yantra*^ for South-East
- Deep Sea Corals *(Specific Patterns Needed)**
- Deep Sea Shells *(Specific Patterns Needed)**
- Protection Bug Fossil^^^
- Pure & Natural Crystal Balls
- Pure Stone Pyramid
- 7 Silver Grey Pyramids
- White Flowers
- Boar Pearl^^^
- Silver & Sparkling White Colors
- Infinity Gem^^ (Faco Crystal) White^^
- Kaama Siyar Singhi
- Jungli Kaali Billi ki Jer*^^
- Kamakhaya Sindhoor
- Negativity Cleaning Crystals
- Salt Lamp
- Bidaal Mani^^^
- 925 Sterling Silver Artifacts
- Rudrakshas:-
  - 1 Mukhi Trinetra Rudraksha^^

> ➤ 1 Mukhi Jyotir Lingum Rudraksha^^
> ➤ 16 Mukhi Rudraksha
> ➤ 20 Mukhi Rudraksha
> ➤ 25 Mukhi Rudraksha^^

Remedies of Mandir / Prayer Room / Puja Room in South

- Directional Healing Crystal for South
- Secret Programmed Vastu Diviner^^ for South
- Specially Formulated Vastu Dosh Nivaran Yantra*^ for South
- Pure Stone Pyramid
- 8 Red Pyramids *
- Negativity Cleaning Crystals
- Salt Lamp
- Red Color
- Venu Mani^^^
- Raw Burmese Ruby
- Boar Pearl^^^
- Protection Bug Fossil^^^
- Red Lord Hanuman Photo / Idol
- Hatha Jodi Actual with Root
- Jungli Kaali Billi ki Jer*^^
- Kamakhaya Sindhoor
- Shwetark Ganpati
- Gaj Mukta^^^
- Jungli Suar ka Daant
- Dakshinavarti Shankh
- Red Gemstones & Crystals:-
  > ➤ Carnelian
  > ➤ Red Garnet
  > ➤ Qabana Stone^^
  > ➤ Red Jasper
  > ➤ Red Agate
  > ➤ Red Fluorite

- ➤ Wolk Stone^^
- ➤ Red Sapphire
- ➤ Red Spinel
- ➤ Red Coral
- ➤ Heart Shaped Coral
- Rudrakshas:-
  - ➤ 17 Mukhi Rudraksha
  - ➤ 19 Mukhi Rudraksha^^
  - ➤ 26 Mukhi Rudraksha^^
  - ➤ 28 Mukhi Rudraksha^^

Remedies of Mandir / Prayer Room / Puja Room in South-West

- Gemstones & Crystals:-
  - ➤ Smokey Quartz
  - ➤ Bronzite
  - ➤ Brown Agates
  - ➤ Grey Agates
  - ➤ Qabana Stone^^
  - ➤ Tiger's Eye Crystal
  - ➤ Amber
  - ➤ Wolk Stone^^
  - ➤ Smokey Topaz
  - ➤ Hessonite Garnet
  - ➤ Grey Japanese Coral
- Directional Healing Crystal for South-West
- Secret Programmed Vastu Diviner^^ for South-West
- Specially Formulated Vastu Dosh Nivaran Yantra*^ for South-West
- Negativity Cleaning Crystals
- Pure Stone Pyramid
- 10 or 11 Brown Pyramids
- Salt Lamp
- Rahu ki Kaudi

- Venu Mani^^^
- Brown & Grey Colors
- Naagmani Glowing^^
- Jungli Kaali Billi ki Jer*^^
- Hatha Jodi Jadh Samet (With Root)
- Brahmajaal
- Protection Bug Fossil^^^
- Boar Pearl^^^
- Parad Shivling
- Shwetark Ganpati
- Talismani Mani for Enemies
- Sher ka Daant
- Shark Teeth
- Gaj Mukta^^^
- Antrikha / Space Stone / Space Stone Antrikha^^^
- Rudrakshas:-
  - ➢ 10 Mukhi Rudraksha
  - ➢ 11 Mukhi Rudraksha
  - ➢ 19 Mukhi Rudraksha
  - ➢ 28 Mukhi Rudraksha^^
  - ➢ 29 Mukhi Rudraksha^^
  - ➢ 1 Mukhi Trinetra Rudraksha^^
  - ➢ 1 Mukhi Jyotir Lingum Rudraksha^^
  - ➢ Charam Pashupati Nath Rudraksha^^^

Remedies of Mandir / Prayer Room / Puja Room in West

- Gemstones & Crystals:-
  - ➢ Lapis Lazuli
  - ➢ Hematite
  - ➢ Angelite
  - ➢ Oyester Pearl^^
  - ➢ Moti Mani^^
  - ➢ Black Obsidian
  - ➢ Blue Tourmaline

- ➢ Aquamarine
- ➢ Blue Agate
- ➢ Black Agate
- ➢ Iolite
- ➢ Conk Stone^^^
- ➢ Sodalite
- ➢ Blue Fluorite
- ➢ Blue Amber
- ➢ Azurite
- ➢ Black Opal
- ➢ Black Pearl
- ➢ Black Onyx
- ➢ Black Tourmaline
- ➢ Kyanite
- ➢ Cordierite
- ➢ Samudrik Stone^^
- ➢ Purple Sapphire
- ➢ Japanese Blue Coral
- ➢ Japanese Black Coral
- ➢ Black Spinel
- Blue Water Pyramid
- Directional Healing Crystal for West
- Secret Programmed Vastu Diviner^^ for West
- Specially Formulated Vastu Dosh Nivaran Yantra*^ for West
- Water Charging Crystals
- Negativity Cleaning Crystals
- Salt Lamp
- Pure Stone Pyramid
- 10 or 11 Black / Blue Pyramids
- Morogul Mani^
- Conk Pearl Gilabi Mani^^^
- Education Tower
- Raw Sugilite Crystal
- Raw Turquoise Crystals
- Black & Blue Colors

- Infinity Gem^^ (Faco Crystal) Green
- Narmadeshwar Shivling Black
- Saam Siyar Singhi
- Jungli Kaali Billi ki Jer*^^
- Hatha Jodi
- Gaj Mukta^^^
- Dakshinavarti Shankh
- Sahastra Sampudh Mani^
- Dhan ka Bandha^
- Samudrik Mani^^
- Rudrakshas:-
  - 10 Mukhi Rudraksha
  - 11 Mukhi Rudraksha
  - 19 Mukhi Rudraksha
  - 28 Mukhi Rudraksha^^
  - 29 Mukhi Rudraksha^^
  - 1 Mukhi Trinetra Rudraksha^^
  - 1 Mukhi Jyotir Lingum Rudraksha^^

Remedies of Mandir / Prayer Room / Puja Room in North-West

- White Gemstones & Crystals:-
  - Clear Quartz
  - White Agate
  - Adra Stone^^
  - White Jade
  - Fully Round Natural Pearl^
  - Mother of Pearl
  - Moonstone
  - Triphane Gemstone^^
- Directional Healing Crystal for North-West
- Secret Programmed Vastu Diviner^^ for North-West
- Negativity Cleaning Crystals
- Salt Lamp

- Megha Mani^^
- Moon Rock^
- Aakash Mani Nubh Mani^^
- Infinity Gem^^ (Faco Crystal) White
- Pearl White Color
- Pure Stone Pyramid
- 4 White Pyramids
- Narmadeshwar Shivling White
- Pearl Blisters
- Protection Bug Fossil^^^
- Bidaal Mani^^^
- Siyar Singhi Joda Male Female Pair
- Rudrakshas:-
  - 4 Mukhi Rudraksha
  - 13 Mukhi Rudraksha
  - 22 Mukhi Rudraksha^
  - 1 Mukhi Trinetra Rudraksha^^
  - 1 Mukhi Jyotir Lingum Rudraksha^^

Remedies of Mandir / Prayer Room / Puja Room in North

- Gemstones & Crystals:-
  - Green Jade
  - Conk Stone^^^
  - Green Aventurine
  - Green Agate
  - Green Garnet
  - Green Tourmaline
  - Peridot
  - Hiddenite^
  - Green Amber
  - Green Turquoise
  - Malachite
  - Oyester Pearl^^
  - Moti Mani^^

- ➢ Green Fluorite
- ➢ Green Jasper
- ➢ Amazonite
- ➢ Florite
- ➢ Samudrik Stone^^
- ➢ Parasha Gemstone^^^
- ➢ Green Tourmaline
- ➢ Green Beryl^
- Green Water Pyramid
- Directional Healing Crystal for North
- Secret Programmed Vastu Diviner^^ for North
- Specially Formulated Vastu Dosh Nivaran Yantra*^ for North
- Water Charging Crystals
- Negativity Cleaning Crystals
- Salt Lamp
- Money Eggs^^
- Infinity Gem^^ (Faco Crystal) Green
- Morogul Mani^
- Green Color
- Plants
- Pure Stone Pyramid
- 3 or 6 Green Pyramids
- Samudrik Mani^^
- Raw Emerald
- Conk Pearl Gilabi Mani^^^
- Indrajaal, Brahmajaal
- Jungli Kaali Billi ki Jer*^^
- Hatha Jodi with Actual Root
- Saam Siyar Singhi
- Sahastra Sampudh Mani^
- Dakshinavarti Shankh
- Dhan ka Bandha*^
- Asphetic Shri Yantra
- Rudrakshas:-

- ➤ 3 Mukhi Rudraksha
- ➤ 6 Mukhi Rudraksha
- ➤ 15 Mukhi Rudraksha
- ➤ 21 Mukhi Rudraksha^
- ➤ 25 Mukhi Rudraksha^^
- ➤ 30 Mukhi Rudraksha^^

Remedies for Staircase

In this section, we have provided the right vastu correction tools and vastu dosh nivaran products to be used to rectify ill effects of staircase in wrong directions.

Remedies for Staircase in North-East
- Directional Healing Crystal for North-East
- Secret Programmed Vastu Diviner *^^ for North-East
- Specially Formulated Vastu Dosh Nivaran Yantra for North East *^
- Water Charging Crystals
- Negativity Cleaning Crystals
- Salt Lamp
- Pure Stone Pyramid
- 9 or 12 Yellow Pyramids
- Yellow Water Pyramid
- Gems & Crystals:-
  - Conk Stone^^^

- ➤ Deep Yellow Citrine
- ➤ Yellow Triphane Gemstone^^
- ➤ Oyester Pearl^^
- ➤ Moti Mani^^
- ➤ Yellow Florspar
- ➤ Yellow Spodumene
- ➤ Yellow Beryl
- ➤ Samudrik Stone^^
- ➤ Golden Yellow Japanese Coral
- Protection Bug Fossil^^^
- Morogul Mani^
- Conk Pearl Gilabi Mani^^^
- Yellow Color
- Antrikha / Space Stone / Space Stone Antrikha*^^^
- Naagmani Glowing^^
- Sahastra Sampudh Mani^
- Parad Shivling
- Samudrik Mani^^
- Rudrakshas:
  - ➤ 12 Mukhi Rudraksha
  - ➤ 18 Mukhi Rudraksha
  - ➤ 27 Mukhi Rudraksha
  - ➤ 1 Mukhi Rudraksha Gole Dana
  - ➤ 21 Mukhi Rudraksha
  - ➤ Combination of 16 Mukhi Rudraksha + 17 Mukhi Rudraksha + 18 Mukhi Rudraksha
- Combination of Kaali Billi ki Jer + Siyar Singhi + Mota Hatha Jodi
- Combination of 120-140 Vastu Healing Products
- Asphetic Shri Yantra

Remedies for Staircase in East

- Gems & Crystals: -
  - ➤ Conk Stone^^^
  - ➤ Oyester Pearl^^

  - ➢ Moti Mani^^
  - ➢ Orange Beryl
  - ➢ Samudrik Stone^^
  - ➢ Amber
- Orange Water Pyramid
- Secret Programmed Vastu Diviner^^ for East
- Specially Formulated Vastu Dosh Nivaran Yantra*^ for East
- Education Tower
- Morogul Mani^
- Sahastra Sampudh Mani^
- Conk Pearl Gilabi Mani^^^
- Infinity Gem^^ (Faco Crystal) Green
- Rudrakshas: -
  - ➢ 1 Mukhi Rudraksha Gole Dana
  - ➢ 21 Mukhi Rudraksha
  - ➢ 14 Mukhi Rudraksha
  - ➢ 23 Mukhi Rudraksha
  - ➢ Combination of 16 Mukhi Rudraksha + 17 Mukhi Rudraksha + 18 Mukhi Rudraksha
- Antrikha / Space Stone Antrikha *^
- Protective Bug
- Naagmani
- Combination of Kaali Billi ki Jer + Siyar Singhi + Mota Hatha Jodi
- Kamakhaya Sindoor
- Parad Shivling
- Combination of 120-140 Vastu Healing Products

Remedies for Staircase in South-East
- Gemstones & Crystals:-
  - ➢ Qabana Stone^^
  - ➢ White Spodumene
  - ➢ Triphane Gemstone^^
  - ➢ White Beryl

- Secret Programmed Vastu Diviner*^^ for South-East
- Specially Formulated Vastu Dosh Nivaran Yantra*^ for South-East
- Deep Sea Corals *(Specific Patterns Needed)*
- Deep Sea Shells *(Specific Patterns Needed)*
- Boar Pearl^^^
- Pure Stone Pyramid
- Protection Bug Fossil^^^
- Negativity Cleaning Crystals
- Bidaal Mani^^^
- Infinity Gem^^ (Faco Crystal) White
- Kaama Siyar Singhi
- Jungli Kaali Billi ki Jer*^^
- Rudrakshas:-
  - 1 Mukhi Rudraksha Gole Dana
  - 21 Mukhi Rudraksha
  - 1 Mukhi Trinetra Rudraksha^^
  - 1 Mukhi Jyotir Lingum Rudraksha^^
  - 16 Mukhi Rudraksha
  - 20 Mukhi Rudraksha
  - 25 Mukhi Rudraksha^^
  - Combination of 16 Mukhi Rudraksha + 17 Mukhi Rudraksha + 18 Mukhi Rudraksha
- Antrikha / Space Stone Antrikha *^
- Naagmani Glowing^^
- Combination of Kaali Billi ki Jer + Siyar Singhi + Mota Hatha Jodi
- Combination of 120-140 Vastu Healing Products

Remedies for Staircase in North-West
- White Gemstones & Crystals:-
  - Adra Stone^^
  - Fully Round Natural Pearl^
  - Triphane Gemstone^^

- Secret Programmed Vastu Diviner^^ for North-West
- Megha Mani^^
- Moon Rock^
- Aakash Mani Nubh Mani^^
- Infinity Gem^^ (Faco Crystal) White
- Pearl Blisters
- Protection Bug Fossil^^^
- Bidaal Mani^^^
- Siyar Singhi Joda Male Female Pair
- Rudrakshas:-
  - 1 Mukhi Rudraksha Gole Dana
  - 21 Mukhi Rudraksha
  - 22 Mukhi Rudraksha^
  - 1 Mukhi Trinetra Rudraksha^^
  - 1 Mukhi Jyotir Lingum Rudraksha^^
  - Combination of 16 Mukhi Rudraksha + 17 Mukhi Rudraksha + 18 Mukhi Rudraksha
- Combination of 120-140 Vastu Healing Products
- Antrikha / Space Stone Antrikha *^
- Naagmani Glowing^^

Remedies for Staircase in North

- Gemstones & Crystals:-
  - Conk Stone^^^
  - Hiddenite^
  - Oyester Pearl^^
  - Moti Mani^^
  - Samudrik Stone^^
  - Parasha Gemstone^^^
  - Green Beryl^
- Secret Programmed Vastu Diviner^^ for North
- Specially Formulated Vastu Dosh Nivaran Yantra*^ for North
- Money Eggs^^

- Infinity Gem^^ (Faco Crystal) Green
- Morogul Mani^
- Samudrik Mani^^
- Raw Emerald
- Conk Pearl Gilabi Mani^^^
- Jungli Kaali Billi ki Jer*^^
- Hatha Jodi with Actual Root
- Saam Siyar Singhi
- Sahastra Sampudh Mani^
- Dhan ka Bandha*^
- Antrikha / Space Stone Antrikha *^
- Protective Bug
- Naagmani Glowing^^^
- Combination of 120-140 Vastu Healing Products
- Kastoori
- Rudrakshas:-
  - ➢ 1 Mukhi Rudraksha Gole Dana
  - ➢ 21 Mukhi Rudraksha
  - ➢ 15 Mukhi Rudraksha
  - ➢ 21 Mukhi Rudraksha^
  - ➢ 25 Mukhi Rudraksha^^
  - ➢ 30 Mukhi Rudraksha^^
  - ➢ Combination of 16 Mukhi Rudraksha + 17 Mukhi Rudraksha + 18 Mukhi Rudraksha

Remedies for Storeroom, Heavy Storage, Large Storage

In this section, we have provided the right vastu correction tools and vastu dosh nivaran products to be used to rectify ill effects of store rooms, heavy storage, large storage in wrong directions.

Remedies for Storeroom in North-East

- Pure Stone Pyramid
- 9 or 12 Yellow Pyramids
- Yellow Water Pyramid
- Gems & Crystals:-
  - ➢ Yellow Jade
  - ➢ Yellow Aventurine
  - ➢ Yellow Jasper
  - ➢ Yellow Garnet
  - ➢ Conk Stone^^^
  - ➢ Deep Yellow Citrine
  - ➢ Yellow Triphane Gemstone^^
  - ➢ Yellow Tourmaline
  - ➢ Yellow Topaz
  - ➢ Yellow Opal

- ➤ Oyester Pearl^^
- ➤ Moti Mani^^
- ➤ Yellow Labradorite
- ➤ Yellow Agate
- ➤ Yellow Florspar
- ➤ Yellow Spodumene
- ➤ Yellow Beryl
- ➤ Scapolite
- ➤ Samudrik Stone^^
- ➤ Golden Yellow Japanese Coral
- Directional Healing Crystal for North-East
- Secret Programmed Vastu Diviner *^^ for North-East
- Specially Formulated Vastu Dosh Nivaran Yantra for North East *^
- Water Charging Crystals
- Negativity Cleaning Crystals
- Salt Lamp
- Indrajaal
- Protection Bug Fossil^^^
- Morogul Mani^
- Conk Pearl Gilabi Mani^^^
- Yellow Color
- Antrikha / Space Stone / Space Stone Antrikha*^^^
- Nav-Grah Pyramid Yantra
- Naagmani Glowing^^
- Kamakhya Sindhoor
- Sahastra Sampudh Mani^
- Parad Shivling
- Samudrik Mani^^
- Shwetark Ganpati
- Haldi ke Ganesh
- Kastoori
- Rudrakshas:-
  - ➤ 1 Mukhi Rudraksha Gole Dana

- ➢ 21 Mukhi Rudraksha
- ➢ 9 Mukhi Rudraksha
- ➢ 12 Mukhi Rudraksha
- ➢ 18 Mukhi Rudraksha
- ➢ 27 Mukhi Rudraksha
- ➢ Combination of 16 Mukhi Rudraksha + 17 Mukhi Rudraksha + 18 Mukhi Rudraksha
- Protective Bug
- Combination of Brahmajaal + Indrajaal
- Combination of Kaali Billi ki Jer + Siyar Singhi + Mota Hatha Jodi
- Combination of 120-140 Vastu Healing Products
- Asphetic Shri Yantra

Remedies for Storeroom in East

- Pure Stone Pyramid
- 5 Orange Pyramids
- Orange Water Pyramid
- Gems & Crystals:-
  - ➢ Orange Sunstone
  - ➢ Orange Topaz
  - ➢ Orange Tourmaline
  - ➢ Orange Garnet
  - ➢ Orange Opal
  - ➢ Conk Stone^^^
  - ➢ Orange Sphalerite
  - ➢ Orange Flourite
  - ➢ Carnelian
  - ➢ Oyester Pearl^^
  - ➢ Moti Mani^^
  - ➢ Orange Agate
  - ➢ Peach Aventurine
  - ➢ Orange Beryl
  - ➢ Orange Citrine
  - ➢ Samudrik Stone^^
  - ➢ Amber

- Directional Healing Crystal for East
- Secret Programmed Vastu Diviner^^ for East
- Specially Formulated Vastu Dosh Nivaran Yantra*^ for East
- Education Tower
- Morogul Mani^
- Sahastra Sampudh Mani^
- Water Charging Crystals
- Negativity Cleaning Crystals
- Salt Lamp
- Conk Pearl Gilabi Mani^^^
- Orange Color
- Infinity Gem^^ (Faco Crystal) Green
- Sher Ka Daant (Lions Teeth)
- Antrikha / Space Stone Antrikha*^^
- Protective Bug
- Naagmani Glowing^^
- Combination of Brahmajaal + Indrajaal
- Combination of Kaali Billi ki Jer + Siyar Singhi + Mota Hatha Jodi
- Kamakhaya Sindoor
- Parad Shivling
- Combination of 120-140 Vastu Healing Products
- Kastoori
- Asphetic Shri Yantra
- Junglee Suar ka Daant (Wild Pig Teeth)
- Rudrakshas:-
  - 1 Mukhi Rudraksha Gole Dana
  - 21 Mukhi Rudraksha
  - 5 Mukhi Rudraksha
  - 14 Mukhi Rudraksha
  - 23 Mukhi Rudraksha
  - Combination of 16 Mukhi Rudraksha + 17 Mukhi Rudraksha + 18 Mukhi Rudraksha

Remedies for Storeroom in South-East

- Gemstones & Crystals:-
  - ➤ Cubic Zirconia
  - ➤ Zircon
  - ➤ Asphetic
  - ➤ Qabana Stone^^
  - ➤ White Topaz
  - ➤ White Spodumene
  - ➤ Opal
  - ➤ Triphane Gemstone^^
  - ➤ White Beryl
- Directional Healing Crystal for South-East
- Secret Programmed Vastu Diviner*^^ for South-East
- Specially Formulated Vastu Dosh Nivaran Yantra*^ for South-East
- Deep Sea Corals *(Specific Patterns Needed)**
- Deep Sea Shells *(Specific Patterns Needed)**
- Pure & Natural Crystal Balls
- White Flowers
- Boar Pearl^^^
- Pure Stone Pyramid
- 7 Grey Pyramids
- Protection Bug Fossil^^^
- Negativity Cleaning Crystals
- Salt Lamp
- Bidaal Mani^^^
- 925 Sterling Silver Artifacts
- Silver & Sparkling White Colors
- Infinity Gem^^ (Faco Crystal) White
- Kaama Siyar Singhi
- Jungli Kaali Billi ki Jer*^^
- Kamakhaya Sindhoor
- Rudraksha:-
  - ➤ 1 Mukhi Rudraksha Gole Dana
  - ➤ 21 Mukhi Rudraksha

- ➤ 1 Mukhi Trinetra Rudraksha^^
- ➤ 1 Mukhi Jyotir Lingum Rudraksha^^
- ➤ 2 Mukhi Rudraksha
- ➤ 7 Mukhi Rudraksha
- ➤ 16 Mukhi Rudraksha
- ➤ 20 Mukhi Rudraksha
- ➤ 25 Mukhi Rudraksha^^
- ➤ Combination of 16 Mukhi Rudraksha + 17 Mukhi Rudraksha + 18 Mukhi Rudraksha
- Antrikha / Space Stone Antrikha *^
- Protective Bug
- Parad Shivling
- Combination of 120-140 Vastu Healing Products
- Kastoori
- Asphetic Shri Yantra
- Naagmani Glowing^^
- Combination of Brahmajaal + Indrajaal
- Combination of Kaali Billi ki Jer + Siyar Singhi + Mota Hatha Jodi

Remedies for Storeroom in West

- Gemstones & Crystals:-
  - ➤ Lapis Lazuli
  - ➤ Hematite
  - ➤ Angelite
  - ➤ Oyester Pearl^^
  - ➤ Moti Mani^^
  - ➤ Black Obsidian
  - ➤ Blue Tourmaline
  - ➤ Aquamarine
  - ➤ Blue Agate
  - ➤ Black Agate
  - ➤ Iolite
  - ➤ Conk Stone^^^
  - ➤ Sodalite

- - Blue Fluorite
  - Blue Amber
  - Azurite
  - Black Opal
  - Black Pearl
  - Black Onyx
  - Black Tourmaline
  - Kyanite
  - Cordierite
  - Samudrik Stone^^
  - Purple Sapphire
  - Japanese Blue Coral
  - Japanese Black Coral
  - Black Spinel
- Pure Stone Pyramid
- 10 or 11 Black / Blue Pyramids
- Blue Water Pyramid
- Directional Healing Crystal for West
- Secret Programmed Vastu Diviner^^ for West
- Specially Formulated Vastu Dosh Nivaran Yantra*^ for West
- Water Charging Crystals
- Negativity Cleaning Crystals
- Salt Lamp
- Morogul Mani^
- Conk Pearl Gilabi Mani^^^
- Education Tower
- Raw Sugilite Crystal
- Raw Turquoise Crystals
- Black & Blue Colors
- Infinity Gem^^ (Faco Crystal) Green
- Narmadeshwar Shivling Black
- Saam Siyar Singhi
- Jungli Kaali Billi ki Jer*^^
- Hatha Jodi
- Gaj Mukta^^^

- Dakshinavarti Shankh
- Sahastra Sampudh Mani^
- Dhan ka Bandha^
- Samudrik Mani^^
- Rudraksha:-
  - 1 Mukhi Rudraksha Gole Dana
  - 21 Mukhi Rudraksha
  - 10 Mukhi Rudraksha
  - 11 Mukhi Rudraksha
  - 19 Mukhi Rudraksha
  - 28 Mukhi Rudraksha^^
  - 29 Mukhi Rudraksha^^
  - 1 Mukhi Trinetra Rudraksha^^
  - 1 Mukhi Jyotir Lingum Rudraksha^^
  - Combination of 16 Mukhi Rudraksha + 17 Mukhi Rudraksha + 18 Mukhi Rudraksha
- Kamakhaya Sindoor
- Parad Shivling
- Combination of 120-140 Vastu Healing Products
- Kastoori
- Asphetic Shri Yantra
- Antrikha / Space Stone Antrikha *^
- Protective Bug
- Naagmani Glowing^^
- Combination of Brahmajaal + Indrajaal
- Combination of Kaali Billi ki Jer + Siyar Singhi + Mota Hatha Jodi

Remedies for Storeroom in North-West

- Directional Healing Crystal for North-West
- Secret Programmed Vastu Diviner^^ for North-West
- Negativity Cleaning Crystals
- Salt Lamp

- Pure Stone Pyramid
- 4 White Pyramids
- White Gemstones & Crystals for North-West:-
  - Clear Quartz
  - White Agate
  - Adra Stone^^
  - White Jade
  - Fully Round Natural Pearl^
  - Mother of Pearl
  - Moonstone
  - Triphane Gemstone^^
- Megha Mani^^
- Moon Rock^
- Aakash Mani Nubh Mani^^
- Infinity Gem^^ (Faco Crystal) White
- Pearl White Color
- Narmadeshwar Shivling White
- Pearl Blisters
- Protection Bug Fossil^^^
- Bidaal Mani^^^
- Siyar Singhi Joda Male Female Pair
- Rudraksha:-
  - 1 Mukhi Rudraksha Gole Dana
  - 21 Mukhi Rudraksha
  - 4 Mukhi Rudraksha
  - 13 Mukhi Rudraksha
  - 22 Mukhi Rudraksha^
  - 1 Mukhi Trinetra Rudraksha^^
  - 1 Mukhi Jyotir Lingum Rudraksha^^
  - Combination of 16 Mukhi Rudraksha + 17 Mukhi Rudraksha + 18 Mukhi Rudraksha
- Antrikha / Space Stone Antrikha *^
- Protective Bug
- Naagmani
- Combination of Brahmajaal + Indrajaal

- Combination of Kaali Billi ki Jer + Siyar Singhi + Mota Hatha Jodi
- Kamakhaya Sindoor
- Parad Shivling
- Combination of 120-140 Vastu Healing Products
- Kastoori
- Asphetic Shri Yantra

Remedies for Storeroom in North

- Gemstones & Crystals for North:-
  - Green Jade
  - Conk Stone^^^
  - Green Aventurine
  - Green Agate
  - Green Garnet
  - Green Tourmaline
  - Peridot
  - Hiddenite^
  - Green Amber
  - Green Turquoise
  - Malachite
  - Oyester Pearl^^
  - Moti Mani^^
  - Green Fluorite
  - Green Jasper
  - Amazonite
  - Florite
  - Samudrik Stone^^
  - Parasha Gemstone^^^
  - Green Tourmaline
  - Green Beryl^
- Green Water Pyramid
- Directional Healing Crystal for North
- Secret Programmed Vastu Diviner^^ for North
- Specially Formulated Vastu Dosh Nivaran Yantra*^ for North

- Water Charging Crystals
- Negativity Cleaning Crystals
- Salt Lamp
- Pure Stone Pyramid
- 3 or 6 Green Pyramids
- Money Eggs^^
- Infinity Gem^^ (Faco Crystal) Green
- Morogul Mani^
- Green Color
- Plants
- Samudrik Mani^^
- Raw Emerald
- Conk Pearl Gilabi Mani^^^
- Indrajaal, Brahmajaal
- Jungli Kaali Billi ki Jer*^^
- Hatha Jodi with Actual Root
- Saam Siyar Singhi
- Sahastra Sampudh Mani^
- Dakshinavarti Shankh
- Dhan ka Bandha*^
- Asphetic Shri Yantra
- Rudraksha:-
  - 1 Mukhi Rudraksha Gole Dana
  - 21 Mukhi Rudraksha
  - 3 Mukhi Rudraksha
  - 6 Mukhi Rudraksha
  - 15 Mukhi Rudraksha
  - 21 Mukhi Rudraksha^
  - 25 Mukhi Rudraksha^^
  - 30 Mukhi Rudraksha^^
  - Combination of 16 Mukhi Rudraksha + 17 Mukhi Rudraksha + 18 Mukhi Rudraksha
- Antrikha / Space Stone Antrikha *^
- Protective Bug
- Naagmani

- Combination of Brahmajaal + Indrajaal
- Combination of Kaali Billi ki Jer + Siyar Singhi + Mota Hatha Jodi
- Combination of 120-140 Vastu Healing Products
- Kastoori
- Asphetic Shri Yantra
- Kamakhaya Sindoor
- Parad Shivling

Remedies for Bedrooms & Master Bedrooms

In this section, we have provided the right vastu correction tools and vastu dosh nivaran products to be used to rectify ill effects of bedrooms and master bedrooms in wrong directions.

Remedies for Bedrooms & Master Bedrooms in North-East

- Gems & Crystals:-
  - ➢ Yellow Jade
  - ➢ Yellow Aventurine
  - ➢ Yellow Jasper
  - ➢ Yellow Garnet
  - ➢ Conk Stone^^^
  - ➢ Deep Yellow Citrine
  - ➢ Yellow Triphane Gemstone^^
  - ➢ Yellow Tourmaline
  - ➢ Yellow Topaz
  - ➢ Yellow Opal

- ➤ Oyester Pearl^^
- ➤ Moti Mani^^
- ➤ Yellow Labradorite
- ➤ Yellow Agate
- ➤ Yellow Florspar
- ➤ Yellow Spodumene
- ➤ Yellow Beryl
- ➤ Scapolite
- ➤ Samudrik Stone^^
- ➤ Golden Yellow Japanese Coral
- 9 or 12 Yellow Pyramids
- Yellow Water Pyramid
- Pure Stone Pyramid
- Directional Healing Crystal for North-East
- Secret Programmed Vastu Diviner *^^ for North-East
- Specially Formulated Vastu Dosh Nivaran Yantra for North East *^
- Water Charging Crystals
- Negativity Cleaning Crystals
- Salt Lamp
- Rudrakshas:-
  - ➤ 9 Mukhi Rudraksha
  - ➤ 12 Mukhi Rudraksha
  - ➤ 18 Mukhi Rudraksha
  - ➤ 27 Mukhi Rudraksha
- Indrajaal
- Protection Bug Fossil^^^
- Morogul Mani^
- Conk Pearl Gilabi Mani^^^
- Yellow Color
- Antrikha / Space Stone / Space Stone Antrikha*^^^
- Nav-Grah Pyramid Yantra
- Naagmani Glowing^^
- Kamakhya Sindhoor

- Sahastra Sampudh Mani^
- Parad Shivling
- Samudrik Mani^^
- Kastoori
- Shwetark Ganpati
- Haldi ke Ganesh

Remedies for Bedrooms & Master Bedrooms in East
- Gems & Crystals:-
  - Orange Sunstone
  - Orange Topaz
  - Orange Tourmaline
  - Orange Garnet
  - Orange Opal
  - Conk Stone^^^
  - Orange Sphalerite
  - Orange Flourite
  - Carnelian
  - Oyester Pearl^^
  - Moti Mani^^
  - Orange Agate
  - Peach Aventurine
  - Orange Beryl
  - Orange Citrine
  - Samudrik Stone^^
  - Amber
- Directional Healing Crystal for East
- Secret Programmed Vastu Diviner^^ for East
- Specially Formulated Vastu Dosh Nivaran Yantra*^ for East
- Morogul Mani^
- Pure Stone Pyramid
- 5 Orange Pyramids
- Orange Water Pyramid
- Sahastra Sampudh Mani^

- Water Charging Crystals
- Negativity Cleaning Crystals
- Conk Pearl Gilabi Mani^^^
- Orange Color
- Infinity Gem^^ (Faco Crystal) Green
- Sher Ka Daant (Lions Teeth)
- Junglee Suar ka Daant (Wild Pig Teeth)
- Rudrakshas:-
  - 5 Mukhi Rudraksha
  - 14 Mukhi Rudraksha
  - 23 Mukhi Rudraksha

Remedies for Bedrooms & Master Bedrooms in South-East

- Gemstones & Crystals:-
  - Cubic Zirconia
  - Zircon
  - Asphetic
  - Qabana Stone^^
  - White Topaz
  - White Spodumene
  - Opal
  - Triphane Gemstone^^
  - White Beryl
- Directional Healing Crystal for South-East
- Secret Programmed Vastu Diviner*^^ for South-East
- Specially Formulated Vastu Dosh Nivaran Yantra*^ for South-East
- Deep Sea Corals *(Specific Patterns Needed)**
- Deep Sea Shells *(Specific Patterns Needed)**
- Pure & Natural Crystal Balls
- White Flowers
- Boar Pearl^^^
- Protection Bug Fossil^^^

- Negativity Cleaning Crystals
- Salt Lamp
- Bidaal Mani^^^
- Kaama Siyar Singhi
- Jungli Kaali Billi ki Jer*^^
- Kamakhaya Sindhoor
- Pure Stone Pyramid
- 7 Grey Pyramids
- 925 Sterling Silver Artifacts
- Rudrakshas:-
  - 1 Mukhi Trinetra Rudraksha^^
  - 1 Mukhi Jyotir Lingum Rudraksha^^
  - 2 Mukhi Rudraksha
  - 7 Mukhi Rudraksha
  - 16 Mukhi Rudraksha
  - 20 Mukhi Rudraksha
  - 25 Mukhi Rudraksha^^
- Silver & Sparkling White Colors
- Infinity Gem^^ (Faco Crystal) White

Remedies for Bedrooms & Master Bedrooms in West

- Gemstones & Crystals:-
  - Lapis Lazuli
  - Hematite
  - Angelite
  - Oyester Pearl^^
  - Moti Mani^^
  - Black Obsidian
  - Blue Tourmaline
  - Aquamarine
  - Blue Agate
  - Black Agate
  - Iolite
  - Conk Stone^^^

- ➢ Sodalite
- ➢ Blue Fluorite
- ➢ Blue Amber
- ➢ Azurite
- ➢ Black Opal
- ➢ Black Pearl
- ➢ Black Onyx
- ➢ Black Tourmaline
- ➢ Kyanite
- ➢ Cordierite
- ➢ Samudrik Stone^^
- ➢ Purple Sapphire
- ➢ Japanese Blue Coral
- ➢ Japanese Black Coral
- ➢ Black Spinel
- Blue Water Pyramid
- Directional Healing Crystal for West
- Secret Programmed Vastu Diviner^^ for West
- Specially Formulated Vastu Dosh Nivaran Yantra*^ for West
- Pure Stone Pyramid
- 10 or 11 Black / Blue Pyramids
- Water Charging Crystals
- Negativity Cleaning Crystals
- Salt Lamp
- Morogul Mani^
- Conk Pearl Gilabi Mani^^^
- Rudrakshas:-
  - ➢ 10 Mukhi Rudraksha
  - ➢ 11 Mukhi Rudraksha
  - ➢ 19 Mukhi Rudraksha
  - ➢ 28 Mukhi Rudraksha^^
  - ➢ 29 Mukhi Rudraksha^^
  - ➢ 1 Mukhi Trinetra Rudraksha^^
  - ➢ 1 Mukhi Jyotir Lingum Rudraksha^^
- Raw Sugilite Crystal

- Raw Turquoise Crystals
- Black & Blue Colors
- Infinity Gem^^ (Faco Crystal) Green
- Narmadeshwar Shivling Black
- Hatha Jodi
- Gaj Mukta^^^
- Sahastra Sampudh Mani^
- Dhan ka Bandha^
- Samudrik Mani^^
- Dakshinavarti Shankh
- Saam Siyar Singhi
- Jungli Kaali Billi ki Jer*^^

Remedies for Bedrooms & Master Bedrooms in North

- Gemstones & Crystals:-
  - Green Jade
  - Conk Stone^^^
  - Green Aventurine
  - Green Agate
  - Green Garnet
  - Green Tourmaline
  - Peridot
  - Hiddenite^
  - Green Amber
  - Green Turquoise
  - Malachite
  - Oyester Pearl^^
  - Moti Mani^^
  - Green Fluorite
  - Green Jasper
  - Amazonite
  - Florite
  - Samudrik Stone^^
  - Parasha Gemstone^^^

- ➤ Green Tourmaline
- ➤ Green Beryl^
- Green Water Pyramid
- Directional Healing Crystal for North
- Secret Programmed Vastu Diviner^^ for North
- Specially Formulated Vastu Dosh Nivaran Yantra*^ for North
- Water Charging Crystals
- Negativity Cleaning Crystals
- Salt Lamp
- Pure Stone Pyramid
- 3 or 6 Green Pyramids
- Rudrakshas:-
  - ➤ 3 Mukhi Rudraksha
  - ➤ 6 Mukhi Rudraksha
  - ➤ 15 Mukhi Rudraksha
  - ➤ 21 Mukhi Rudraksha^
  - ➤ 25 Mukhi Rudraksha^^
  - ➤ 30 Mukhi Rudraksha^^
- Infinity Gem^^ (Faco Crystal) Green
- Morogul Mani^
- Green Color
- Plants
- Samudrik Mani^^
- Raw Emerald
- Conk Pearl Gilabi Mani^^^
- Indrajaal, Brahmajaal
- Jungli Kaali Billi ki Jer*^^
- Hatha Jodi with Actual Root
- Saam Siyar Singhi
- Sahastra Sampudh Mani^
- Dakshinavarti Shankh
- Dhan ka Bandha*^
- Asphetic Shri Yantra

Remedies for Bedrooms & Master Bedrooms in Bhrahmasthan

- Secret Programmed Vastu Diviner^^ for Brahmasthaan
- Specially Formulated Vastu Dosh Nivaran Yantra^^ for Brahmasthaan
- Kale Ghodhe ki Naal
- Nav-Grah Pyramid Yantra
- Rudraksha for Bhrahmasthan:-
  - ➢ 1 Mukhi Rudraksha Gole Dana
  - ➢ 21 Mukhi Rudraksha
  - ➢ Combination of 16 Mukhi Rudraksha + 17 Mukhi Rudraksha + 18 Mukhi Rudraksha
- Antrikha / Space Stone / Space Stone Antrikha^^^
- Infinity Gem^^ (Faco Crystal) White & Green
- Vishnu Chakra Moti^^
- Combination of 20-140 Vastu Items & Products
- Fully Round Natural Pearl^^
- Tutmak Stone^^
- Timi Stone^^^
- Adra Stone^^
- Enemy Stone^^
- **Conk Stone^^^**
- Qabana Stone^^^
- Protection Bug Fossil^^^
- Eagle Stone^^^
- Triphane Gemstone ^^
- Cordierite^^
- Nagmani Black^
- Naagmani Glowing^^^
- Combination of Brahmajaal + Indrajaal
- Combination of Kaali Billi ki Jer + Siyar Singhi + Mota Hatha Jodi
- Kamakhaya Sindoor
- Parad Shivling

- Deep Sea Corals^
- Deep Sea Shells^
- Money Eggs^^
- Combination of 120-140 Vastu Healing Products
- Kastoori
- Asphetic Shri Yantra
- Gemstones for Brahmasthaan: Hiddenite, Parasha, Green Beryl, Green Florite, Yellow Florspar, Yellow Beryl, Yellow Spodumene, Scapolite, White Beryl
- Dhan ka Bandha*^
- Moon Rock^^
- Natural Pearl Blisters
- Rudraksha for Bhrahmasthan:-
  - 1 Mukhi Rudraksha Gole Dana
  - 21 Mukhi Rudraksha
  - Combination of 16 Mukhi Rudraksha + 17 Mukhi Rudraksha + 18 Mukhi Rudraksha
  - 1 Mukhi Java Rudraksha^^
  - 1 Mukhi Java Rudraksha Gehuaan Dana^^
  - Charam Pashupati Nath Rudraksha

Remedies for Bedroom of Newly Wed Couple

In this section, we have provided the right vastu correction tools and vastu dosh nivaran products to be used to rectify ill effects of bedroom of newly wed couple in wrong directions.

Remedies for Bedroom of Newly Wed Couple in North-East

- Gems & Crystals:-
  - ➤ Yellow Jade
  - ➤ Yellow Aventurine
  - ➤ Yellow Jasper
  - ➤ Yellow Garnet
  - ➤ Conk Stone^^^
  - ➤ Deep Yellow Citrine
  - ➤ Yellow Triphane Gemstone^^
  - ➤ Yellow Tourmaline

- ➢ Yellow Topaz
- ➢ Yellow Opal
- ➢ Oyester Pearl^^
- ➢ Moti Mani^^
- ➢ Yellow Labradorite
- ➢ Yellow Agate
- ➢ Yellow Florspar
- ➢ Yellow Spodumene
- ➢ Yellow Beryl
- ➢ Scapolite
- ➢ Samudrik Stone^^
- ➢ Golden Yellow Japanese Coral
- 9 or 12 Yellow Pyramids
- Yellow Water Pyramid
- Pure Stone Pyramid
- Directional Healing Crystal for North-East
- Secret Programmed Vastu Diviner *^^ for North-East
- Specially Formulated Vastu Dosh Nivaran Yantra for North East *^
- Water Charging Crystals
- Negativity Cleaning Crystals
- Salt Lamp
- Rudrakshas:-
  - ➢ 9 Mukhi Rudraksha
  - ➢ 12 Mukhi Rudraksha
  - ➢ 18 Mukhi Rudraksha
  - ➢ 27 Mukhi Rudraksha
- Indrajaal
- Protection Bug Fossil^^^
- Morogul Mani^
- Conk Pearl Gilabi Mani^^^
- Yellow Color
- Antrikha / Space Stone / Space Stone Antrikha*^^^
- Nav-Grah Pyramid Yantra

- Naagmani Glowing^^
- Kamakhya Sindhoor
- Sahastra Sampudh Mani^
- Parad Shivling
- Samudrik Mani^^
- Shwetark Ganpati
- Haldi ke Ganesh
- Kastoori

Remedies for Bedroom of Newly Wed Couple in East
- Gems & Crystals for East Direction:-
  - Orange Sunstone
  - Orange Topaz
  - Orange Tourmaline
  - Orange Garnet
  - Orange Opal
  - Conk Stone^^^
  - Orange Sphalerite
  - Orange Flourite
  - Carnelian
  - Oyester Pearl^^
  - Moti Mani^^
  - Orange Agate
  - Peach Aventurine
  - Orange Beryl
  - Orange Citrine
  - Samudrik Stone^^
  - Amber
- Directional Healing Crystal for East
- Secret Programmed Vastu Diviner^^ for East
- Specially Formulated Vastu Dosh Nivaran Yantra*^ for East
- Morogul Mani^
- Pure Stone Pyramid
- 5 Orange Pyramids
- Orange Water Pyramid

- Sahastra Sampudh Mani^
- Rudrakshas for East:-
  - ➤ 5 Mukhi Rudraksha
  - ➤ 14 Mukhi Rudraksha
  - ➤ 23 Mukhi Rudraksha
- Orange Color
- Infinity Gem^^ (Faco Crystal) Green
- Sher Ka Daant (Lions Teeth)
- Junglee Suar ka Daant (Wild Pig Teeth)
- Water Charging Crystals
- Negativity Cleaning Crystals
- Conk Pearl Gilabi Mani^^^

Remedies for Bedroom of Newly Wed Couple in South East

- Gemstones & Crystals:-
  - ➤ Cubic Zirconia
  - ➤ Zircon
  - ➤ Asphetic
  - ➤ Qabana Stone^^
  - ➤ White Topaz
  - ➤ White Spodumene
  - ➤ Opal
  - ➤ Triphane Gemstone^^
  - ➤ White Beryl
- Directional Healing Crystal for South-East
- Secret Programmed Vastu Diviner*^^ for South-East
- Specially Formulated Vastu Dosh Nivaran Yantra*^ for South-East
- Deep Sea Corals *(Specific Patterns Needed)**
- Deep Sea Shells *(Specific Patterns Needed)**
- Pure & Natural Crystal Balls
- White Flowers
- Boar Pearl^^^

- Rudrakshas:-
  - 1 Mukhi Trinetra Rudraksha^^
  - 1 Mukhi Jyotir Lingum Rudraksha^^
  - 2 Mukhi Rudraksha
  - 7 Mukhi Rudraksha
  - 16 Mukhi Rudraksha
  - 20 Mukhi Rudraksha
  - 25 Mukhi Rudraksha^^
- Silver & Sparkling White Colors
- Infinity Gem^^ (Faco Crystal) White
- Kaama Siyar Singhi
- Jungli Kaali Billi ki Jer*^^
- Kamakhaya Sindhoor
- Protection Bug Fossil^^^
- Negativity Cleaning Crystals
- Salt Lamp
- Bidaal Mani^^^
- Pure Stone Pyramid
- 7 Grey Pyramids
- 925 Sterling Silver Artifacts

Remedies for Bedroom of Newly Wed Couple in South

- Pure Stone Pyramid
- 8 Red Pyramids *
- Red Gemstones & Crystals:-
  - Carnelian
  - Red Garnet
  - Qabana Stone^^
  - Red Jasper
  - Red Agate
  - Red Fluorite
  - Wolk Stone^^
  - Red Sapphire
  - Red Spinel

- ➤ Red Coral
- ➤ Heart Shaped Coral
- Directional Healing Crystal for South
- Secret Programmed Vastu Diviner^^ for South
- Specially Formulated Vastu Dosh Nivaran Yantra*^ for South
- Negativity Cleaning Crystals
- Salt Lamp
- Rudrakshas:-
  - ➤ 1 Mukhi Rudraksha
  - ➤ 8 Mukhi Rudraksha
  - ➤ 17 Mukhi Rudraksha
  - ➤ 19 Mukhi Rudraksha^^
  - ➤ 26 Mukhi Rudraksha^^
  - ➤ 28 Mukhi Rudraksha^^
- Red Color
- Venu Mani^^^
- Raw Burmese Ruby
- Boar Pearl^^^
- Jungli Suar ka Daant
- Dakshinavarti Shankh
- Protection Bug Fossil^^^
- Red Lord Hanuman Photo / Idol
- Hatha Jodi Actual with Root
- Jungli Kaali Billi ki Jer*^^
- Kamakhaya Sindhoor
- Shwetark Ganpati
- Gaj Mukta^^^

Remedies for Bedroom of Newly Wed Couple in South-West

- Pure Stone Pyramid
- 10 or 11 Brown Pyramids

111

- Gemstones & Crystals:-
  - Smokey Quartz
  - Bronzite
  - Brown Agates
  - Grey Agates
  - Qabana Stone^^
  - Tiger's Eye Crystal
  - Amber
  - Wolk Stone^^
  - Smokey Topaz
  - Hessonite Garnet
  - Grey Japanese Coral
- Directional Healing Crystal for South-West
- Secret Programmed Vastu Diviner^^ for South-West
- Specially Formulated Vastu Dosh Nivaran Yantra*^ for South-West
- Negativity Cleaning Crystals
- Salt Lamp
- Rudrakshas:-
  - 10 Mukhi Rudraksha
  - 11 Mukhi Rudraksha
  - 19 Mukhi Rudraksha
  - 28 Mukhi Rudraksha^^
  - 29 Mukhi Rudraksha^^
  - 1 Mukhi Trinetra Rudraksha^^
  - 1 Mukhi Jyotir Lingum Rudraksha^^
  - Charam Pashupati Nath Rudraksha^^^
- Rahu ki Kaudi
- Venu Mani^^^
- Brown & Grey Colors
- Naagmani Glowing^^
- Jungli Kaali Billi ki Jer*^^
- Hatha Jodi Jadh Samet (With Root)
- Sher ka Daant
- Shark Teeth

- Gaj Mukta^^^
- Antrikha / Space Stone / Space Stone Antrikha^^^
- Brahmajaal
- Protection Bug Fossil^^^
- Boar Pearl^^^
- Parad Shivling
- Shwetark Ganpati
- Talismani Mani for Enemies

Remedies for Bedroom of Newly Wed Couple in West

- Gemstones & Crystals:-
  - ➢ Lapis Lazuli
  - ➢ Hematite
  - ➢ Angelite
  - ➢ Oyester Pearl^^
  - ➢ Moti Mani^^
  - ➢ Black Obsidian
  - ➢ Blue Tourmaline
  - ➢ Aquamarine
  - ➢ Blue Agate
  - ➢ Black Agate
  - ➢ Iolite
  - ➢ Conk Stone^^^
  - ➢ Sodalite
  - ➢ Blue Fluorite
  - ➢ Blue Amber
  - ➢ Azurite
  - ➢ Black Opal
  - ➢ Black Pearl
  - ➢ Black Onyx
  - ➢ Black Tourmaline
  - ➢ Kyanite
  - ➢ Cordierite

- - Samudrik Stone^^
  - Purple Sapphire
  - Japanese Blue Coral
  - Japanese Black Coral
  - Black Spinel
- Blue Water Pyramid
- Directional Healing Crystal for West
- Secret Programmed Vastu Diviner^^ for West
- Specially Formulated Vastu Dosh Nivaran Yantra*^ for West
- Pure Stone Pyramid
- 10 or 11 Black / Blue Pyramids
- Water Charging Crystals
- Negativity Cleaning Crystals
- Salt Lamp
- Morogul Mani^
- Conk Pearl Gilabi Mani^^^
- Rudraksha:-
  - 10 Mukhi Rudraksha
  - 11 Mukhi Rudraksha
  - 19 Mukhi Rudraksha
  - 28 Mukhi Rudraksha^^
  - 29 Mukhi Rudraksha^^
  - 1 Mukhi Trinetra Rudraksha^^
  - 1 Mukhi Jyotir Lingum Rudraksha^^
- Raw Sugilite Crystal
- Raw Turquoise Crystals
- Black & Blue Colors
- Infinity Gem^^ (Faco Crystal) Green
- Narmadeshwar Shivling Black
- Saam Siyar Singhi
- Jungli Kaali Billi ki Jer*^^
- Hatha Jodi
- Gaj Mukta^^^
- Dakshinavarti Shankh

- Sahastra Sampudh Mani^
- Dhan ka Bandha^
- Samudrik Mani^^

Remedies for Bedroom of Newly Wed Couple in North

- Gemstones & Crystals:-
  - ➤ Green Jade
  - ➤ Conk Stone^^^
  - ➤ Green Aventurine
  - ➤ Green Agate
  - ➤ Green Garnet
  - ➤ Green Tourmaline
  - ➤ Peridot
  - ➤ Hiddenite^
  - ➤ Green Amber
  - ➤ Green Turquoise
  - ➤ Malachite
  - ➤ Oyester Pearl^^
  - ➤ Moti Mani^^
  - ➤ Green Fluorite
  - ➤ Green Jasper
  - ➤ Amazonite
  - ➤ Florite
  - ➤ Samudrik Stone^^
  - ➤ Parasha Gemstone^^^
  - ➤ Green Tourmaline
  - ➤ Green Beryl^
- Green Water Pyramid
- Directional Healing Crystal for North
- Secret Programmed Vastu Diviner^^ for North
- Specially Formulated Vastu Dosh Nivaran Yantra*^ for North
- Water Charging Crystals
- Negativity Cleaning Crystals

115

- Salt Lamp
- Pure Stone Pyramid
- 3 or 6 Green Pyramids
- Rudraksha:-
  - ➢ 3 Mukhi Rudraksha
  - ➢ 6 Mukhi Rudraksha
  - ➢ 15 Mukhi Rudraksha
  - ➢ 21 Mukhi Rudraksha^
  - ➢ 25 Mukhi Rudraksha^^
  - ➢ 30 Mukhi Rudraksha^^
- Money Eggs^^
- Infinity Gem^^ (Faco Crystal) Green
- Morogul Mani^
- Green Color
- Plants
- Samudrik Mani^^
- Raw Emerald
- Conk Pearl Gilabi Mani^^^
- Indrajaal, Brahmajaal
- Jungli Kaali Billi ki Jer*^^
- Hatha Jodi with Actual Root
- Saam Siyar Singhi
- Sahastra Sampudh Mani^
- Dakshinavarti Shankh
- Dhan ka Bandha*^
- Asphetic Shri Yantra

Remedies for Bedroom of Newly Wed Couple in Bhrahmasthan

- Secret Programmed Vastu Diviner^^ for Brahmasthaan
- Specially Formulated Vastu Dosh Nivaran Yantra^^ for Brahmasthaan
- Kale Ghodhe ki Naal
- Nav-Grah Pyramid Yantra

- Antrikha / Space Stone / Space Stone Antrikha^^^
- Infinity Gem^^ (Faco Crystal) White & Green
- Vishnu Chakra Moti^^
- Combination of 20-140 Vastu Items & Products
- Fully Round Natural Pearl^^
- Tutmak Stone^^
- Timi Stone^^^
- Adra Stone^^
- Enemy Stone^^
- **Conk Stone^^^**
- Qabana Stone^^^
- Protection Bug Fossil^^^
- Eagle Stone^^^
- Triphane Gemstone ^^
- Cordierite^^
- Nagmani Black^
- Naagmani Glowing^^^
- Combination of Brahmajaal + Indrajaal
- Combination of Kaali Billi ki Jer + Siyar Singhi + Mota Hatha Jodi
- Kamakhaya Sindoor
- Parad Shivling
- Deep Sca Corals^
- Deep Sea Shells^
- Money Eggs^^
- Combination of 120-140 Vastu Healing Products
- Kastoori
- Asphetic Shri Yantra
- Dhan ka Bandha*^
- Moon Rock^^
- Natural Pearl Blisters

Remedies of Bedroom of Head of the Family & Administrator of the House

In this section, we have provided the right vastu correction tools and vastu dosh nivaran products to be used to rectify ill effects of bedroom of head of the family in wrong directions.

Remedies of Bedroom of Head of the Family in North-East

- 9 or 12 Yellow Pyramids
- Yellow Water Pyramid
- Pure Stone Pyramid
- Directional Healing Crystal for North-East
- Secret Programmed Vastu Diviner *^^ for North-East
- Specially Formulated Vastu Dosh Nivaran Yantra for North East *^
- Water Charging Crystals
- Negativity Cleaning Crystals

- Salt Lamp
- Indrajaal
- Protection Bug Fossil^^^
- Morogul Mani^
- Conk Pearl Gilabi Mani^^^
- Yellow Color
- Antrikha / Space Stone / Space Stone Antrikha*^^^
- Nav-Grah Pyramid Yantra
- Naagmani Glowing^^
- Kamakhya Sindhoor
- Sahastra Sampudh Mani^
- Parad Shivling
- Samudrik Mani^^
- Shwetark Ganpati
- Haldi ke Ganesh
- Kastoori

Remedies of Bedroom of Head of the Family in East
- Directional Healing Crystal for East
- Secret Programmed Vastu Diviner^^ for East
- Specially Formulated Vastu Dosh Nivaran Yantra*^ for East
- Morogul Mani^
- Pure Stone Pyramid
- 5 Orange Pyramids
- Orange Water Pyramid
- Sahastra Sampudh Mani^
- Water Charging Crystals
- Negativity Cleaning Crystals
- Salt Lamp
- Conk Pearl Gilabi Mani^^^
- Orange Color
- Infinity Gem^^ (Faco Crystal) Green

- Sher Ka Daant (Lions Teeth)
- Junglee Suar ka Daant (Wild Pig Teeth)

Remedies of Bedroom of Head of the Family in South-East

- Directional Healing Crystal for South-East
- Secret Programmed Vastu Diviner*^^ for South-East
- Specially Formulated Vastu Dosh Nivaran Yantra*^ for South-East
- Deep Sea Corals *(Specific Patterns Needed)*
- Deep Sea Shells *(Specific Patterns Needed)*
- Pure & Natural Crystal Balls
- White Flowers
- Boar Pearl^^^
- Protection Bug Fossil^^^
- Negativity Cleaning Crystals
- Salt Lamp
- Bidaal Mani^^^
- Pure Stone Pyramid
- 7 Grey Pyramids
- 925 Sterling Silver Artifacts
- Silver & Sparkling White Colors
- Infinity Gem^^ (Faco Crystal) White
- Kaama Siyar Singhi
- Jungli Kaali Billi ki Jer*^^
- Kamakhaya Sindhoor

Remedies of Bedroom of Head of the Family in South

- Directional Healing Crystal for South
- Secret Programmed Vastu Diviner^^ for South

- Specially Formulated Vastu Dosh Nivaran Yantra*^ for South
- Negativity Cleaning Crystals
- Salt Lamp
- Pure Stone Pyramid
- 8 Red Pyramids *
- Red Color
- Venu Mani^^^
- Raw Burmese Ruby
- Boar Pearl^^^
- Protection Bug Fossil^^^
- Red Lord Hanuman Photo / Idol
- Hatha Jodi Actual with Root
- Jungli Kaali Billi ki Jer*^^
- Kamakhaya Sindhoor
- Shwetark Ganpati
- Gaj Mukta^^^
- Jungli Suar ka Daant
- Dakshinavarti Shankh

Remedies of Bedroom of Head of the Family in West
- Blue Water Pyramid
- Directional Healing Crystal for West
- Secret Programmed Vastu Diviner^^ for West
- Specially Formulated Vastu Dosh Nivaran Yantra*^ for West
- Pure Stone Pyramid
- 10 or 11 Black / Blue Pyramids
- Water Charging Crystals
- Negativity Cleaning Crystals
- Salt Lamp
- Morogul Mani^
- Conk Pearl Gilabi Mani^^^

- Raw Sugilite Crystal
- Raw Turquoise Crystals
- Black & Blue Colors
- Infinity Gem^^ (Faco Crystal) Green
- Narmadeshwar Shivling Black
- Saam Siyar Singhi
- Jungli Kaali Billi ki Jer*^^
- Hatha Jodi
- Gaj Mukta^^^
- Dakshinavarti Shankh
- Sahastra Sampudh Mani^
- Dhan ka Bandha^
- Samudrik Mani^^

Remedies of Bedroom of Head of the Family in North-West

- Pure Stone Pyramid
- 4 White Pyramids
- Directional Healing Crystal for North-West
- Secret Programmed Vastu Diviner^^ for North-West
- Negativity Cleaning Crystals
- Salt Lamp
- Megha Mani^^
- Moon Rock^
- Aakash Mani Nubh Mani^^
- Infinity Gem^^ (Faco Crystal) White
- Pearl White Color
- Narmadeshwar Shivling White
- Pearl Blisters
- Protection Bug Fossil^^^
- Bidaal Mani^^^
- Siyar Singhi Joda Male Female Pair

Remedies of Bedroom of Head of the Family in North

- Green Water Pyramid
- Directional Healing Crystal for North
- Secret Programmed Vastu Diviner^^ for North
- Specially Formulated Vastu Dosh Nivaran Yantra*^ for North
- Water Charging Crystals
- Negativity Cleaning Crystals
- Salt Lamp
- Pure Stone Pyramid
- 3 or 6 Green Pyramids
- Money Eggs^^
- Infinity Gem^^ (Faco Crystal) Green
- Morogul Mani^
- Green Color
- Plants
- Samudrik Mani^^
- Raw Emerald
- Conk Pearl Gilabi Mani^^^
- Indrajaal, Brahmajaal
- Jungli Kaali Billi ki Jer*^^
- Hatha Jodi with Actual Root
- Saam Siyar Singhi
- Sahastra Sampudh Mani^
- Dakshinavarti Shankh
- Dhan ka Bandha*^
- Asphetic Shri Yantra

Remedies of Bedroom of Head of the Family in Bhrahmasthan

- Secret Programmed Vastu Diviner^^ for Brahmasthaan

- Specially Formulated Vastu Dosh Nivaran Yantra^^ for Brahmasthaan
- Kale Ghodhe ki Naal
- Nav-Grah Pyramid Yantra
- Antrikha / Space Stone / Space Stone Antrikha^^^
- Infinity Gem^^ (Faco Crystal) White & Green
- Vishnu Chakra Moti^^
- Combination of 20-140 Vastu Items & Products
- Fully Round Natural Pearl^^
- Tutmak Stone^^
- Timi Stone^^^
- Adra Stone^^
- Enemy Stone^^
- **Conk Stone^^^**
- Qabana Stone^^^
- Protection Bug Fossil^^^
- Eagle Stone^^^
- Triphane Gemstone ^^
- Cordierite^^
- Nagmani Black^
- Naagmani Glowing^^^
- Combination of Brahmajaal + Indrajaal
- Combination of Kaali Billi ki Jer + Siyar Singhi + Mota Hatha Jodi
- Kamakhaya Sindoor
- Parad Shivling Kastoori
- Asphetic Shri Yantra
- Dhan ka Bandha*^
- Moon Rock^^
- Natural Pearl Blisters
- Deep Sea Corals^
- Deep Sea Shells^
- Money Eggs^^
- Combination of 120-140 Vastu Healing Products

Remedies for Bedroom of Unmarried Girl

In this section, we have provided the right vastu correction tools and vastu dosh nivaran products to be used to rectify ill effects of bedroom of unmarried girl in wrong directions.

Remedies for Bedroom of Unmarried Girls in North-East

- 9 or 12 Yellow Pyramids
- Yellow Water Pyramid
- Pure Stone Pyramid
- Directional Healing Crystal for North-East
- Secret Programmed Vastu Diviner *^^ for North-East
- Specially Formulated Vastu Dosh Nivaran Yantra for North East *^
- Water Charging Crystals
- Negativity Cleaning Crystals
- Salt Lamp

- Indrajaal
- Protection Bug Fossil^^^
- Morogul Mani^
- Conk Pearl Gilabi Mani^^^
- Yellow Color
- Antrikha / Space Stone / Space Stone Antrikha*^^^
- Nav-Grah Pyramid Yantra
- Naagmani Glowing^^
- Kamakhya Sindhoor
- Sahastra Sampudh Mani^
- Parad Shivling
- Samudrik Mani^^
- Shwetark Ganpati
- Haldi ke Ganesh
- Kastoori

Remedies for Bedroom of Unmarried Girls in East

- Directional Healing Crystal for East
- Secret Programmed Vastu Diviner^^ for East
- Specially Formulated Vastu Dosh Nivaran Yantra*^ for East
- Education Tower
- Morogul Mani^
- Pure Stone Pyramid
- 5 Orange Pyramids
- Orange Water Pyramid
- Sahastra Sampudh Mani^
- Water Charging Crystals
- Negativity Cleaning Crystals
- Salt Lamp
- Conk Pearl Gilabi Mani^^^
- Orange Color

THE GREAT BIBLE OF "REMEDIAL VASTU"

- Infinity Gem^^ (Faco Crystal) Green
- Sher Ka Daant (Lions Teeth)
- Junglee Suar ka Daant (Wild Pig Teeth)

Remedies for Bedroom of Unmarried Girls in South-East

- Directional Healing Crystal for South-East
- Secret Programmed Vastu Diviner*^^ for South-East
- Specially Formulated Vastu Dosh Nivaran Yantra*^ for South-East
- Deep Sea Corals *(Specific Patterns Needed)**
- Deep Sea Shells *(Specific Patterns Needed)**
- Pure & Natural Crystal Balls
- White Flowers
- Boar Pearl^^^
- Protection Bug Fossil^^^
- Negativity Cleaning Crystals
- Salt Lamp
- Bidaal Mani^^^
- Pure Stone Pyramid
- 7 Grey Pyramids
- 925 Sterling Silver Artifacts
- Silver & Sparkling White Colors
- Infinity Gem^^ (Faco Crystal) White
- Kaama Siyar Singhi
- Jungli Kaali Billi ki Jer*^^
- Kamakhaya Sindhoor

Remedies for Bedroom of Unmarried Girls in South

- Directional Healing Crystal for South
- Secret Programmed Vastu Diviner^^ for South

- Specially Formulated Vastu Dosh Nivaran Yantra*^ for South
- Negativity Cleaning Crystals
- Salt Lamp
- Pure Stone Pyramid
- 8 Red Pyramids *
- Red Color
- Venu Mani^^^
- Raw Burmese Ruby
- Boar Pearl^^^
- Protection Bug Fossil^^^
- Red Lord Hanuman Photo / Idol
- Hatha Jodi Actual with Root
- Jungli Kaali Billi ki Jer*^^
- Gaj Mukta^^^
- Jungli Suar ka Daant
- Dakshinavarti Shankh
- Kamakhaya Sindhoor
- Shwetark Ganpati

Remedies for Bedroom of Unmarried Girls in South-West

- Directional Healing Crystal for South-West
- Secret Programmed Vastu Diviner^^ for South-West
- Specially Formulated Vastu Dosh Nivaran Yantra*^ for South-West
- Negativity Cleaning Crystals
- Salt Lamp
- Pure Stone Pyramid
- 10 or 11 Brown Pyramids
- Rahu ki Kaudi
- Venu Mani^^^

- Brown & Grey Colors
- Naagmani Glowing^^
- Jungli Kaali Billi ki Jer*^^
- Hatha Jodi Jadh Samet (With Root)
- Brahmajaal
- Protection Bug Fossil^^^
- Boar Pearl^^^
- Parad Shivling
- Shwetark Ganpati
- Talismani Mani for Enemies
- Antrikha / Space Stone / Space Stone Antrikha^^^
- Sher ka Daant
- Shark Teeth
- Gaj Mukta^^^

Remedies for Bedroom of Unmarried Girls in West

- Blue Water Pyramid
- Directional Healing Crystal for West
- Secret Programmed Vastu Diviner^^ for West
- Specially Formulated Vastu Dosh Nivaran Yantra*^ for West
- Pure Stone Pyramid
- 10 or 11 Black / Blue Pyramids
- Water Charging Crystals
- Negativity Cleaning Crystals
- Salt Lamp
- Morogul Mani^
- Conk Pearl Gilabi Mani^^^
- Education Tower
- Raw Sugilite Crystal
- Raw Turquoise Crystals
- Black & Blue Colors
- Infinity Gem^^ (Faco Crystal) Green

- Narmadeshwar Shivling Black
- Saam Siyar Singhi
- Jungli Kaali Billi ki Jer*^^
- Hatha Jodi
- Gaj Mukta^^^
- Dakshinavarti Shankh
- Sahastra Sampudh Mani^
- Dhan ka Bandha^
- Samudrik Mani^^

Remedies for Bedroom of Unmarried Girls in North

- Green Water Pyramid
- Directional Healing Crystal for North
- Secret Programmed Vastu Diviner^^ for North
- Specially Formulated Vastu Dosh Nivaran Yantra*^ for North
- Water Charging Crystals
- Negativity Cleaning Crystals
- Salt Lamp
- Pure Stone Pyramid
- 3 or 6 Green Pyramids
- Money Eggs^^
- Infinity Gem^^ (Faco Crystal) Green
- Morogul Mani^
- Green Color
- Plants
- Samudrik Mani^^
- Raw Emerald
- Conk Pearl Gilabi Mani^^^
- Indrajaal, Brahmajaal
- Jungli Kaali Billi ki Jer*^^
- Hatha Jodi with Actual Root

- Saam Siyar Singhi
- Sahastra Sampudh Mani^
- Dakshinavarti Shankh
- Dhan ka Bandha*^
- Asphetic Shri Yantra

Remedies for Bedroom of Unmarried Girls in Bhrahmasthan

- Secret Programmed Vastu Diviner^^ for Brahmasthaan
- Specially Formulated Vastu Dosh Nivaran Yantra^^ for Brahmasthaan
- Kale Ghodhe ki Naal
- Nav-Grah Pyramid Yantra
- Antrikha / Space Stone / Space Stone Antrikha^^^
- Infinity Gem^^ (Faco Crystal) White & Green
- Vishnu Chakra Moti^^
- Combination of 20-140 Vastu Items & Products
- Fully Round Natural Pearl^^
- Tutmak Stone^^
- Timi Stone^^^
- Adra Stone^^
- Enemy Stone^^
- **Conk Stone^^^**
- Qabana Stone^^^
- Protection Bug Fossil^^^
- Eagle Stone^^^
- Triphane Gemstone ^^
- Cordierite^^
- Nagmani Black^
- Naagmani Glowing^^^
- Combination of Brahmajaal + Indrajaal
- Combination of Kaali Billi ki Jer + Siyar Singhi + Mota Hatha Jodi

- Kamakhaya Sindoor
- Parad Shivling
- Deep Sea Corals^
- Deep Sea Shells^
- Money Eggs^^
- Combination of 120-140 Vastu Healing Products
- Kastoori
- Asphetic Shri Yantra
- Dhan ka Bandha*^
- Moon Rock^^
- Natural Pearl Blisters

Remedies for Study Room & Children Room

In this section, we have provided the right vastu correction tools and vastu dosh nivaran products to be used to rectify ill effects of study room and children room in wrong directions.

Remedies for Study Room & Children's Room in North-East

- Gems & Crystals:-
  - ➤ Yellow Jade
  - ➤ Yellow Aventurine
  - ➤ Yellow Jasper
  - ➤ Yellow Garnet
  - ➤ Conk Stone^^^
  - ➤ Deep Yellow Citrine
  - ➤ Yellow Triphane Gemstone^^
  - ➤ Yellow Tourmaline
  - ➤ Yellow Topaz
  - ➤ Yellow Opal

- ➢ Oyester Pearl^^
- ➢ Moti Mani^^
- ➢ Yellow Labradorite
- ➢ Yellow Agate
- ➢ Yellow Florspar
- ➢ Yellow Spodumene
- ➢ Yellow Beryl
- ➢ Scapolite
- ➢ Samudrik Stone^^
- ➢ Golden Yellow Japanese Coral
- Secret Programmed Vastu Diviner^^ for West
- Specially Formulated Vastu Dosh Nivaran Yantra*^ for West
- Education Tower
- Naagmani Glowing^^
- Protection Bug Fossil^^^
- Antrikha / Space Stone / Space Stone Antrikha^^^
- Infinity Gem^^ (Faco Crystal) Green
- Rudrakshas:-
  - ➢ 9 Mukhi Rudraksha
  - ➢ 12 Mukhi Rudraksha
  - ➢ 18 Mukhi Rudraksha
  - ➢ 27 Mukhi Rudraksha

Remedies for Study Room & Children's Room in South-East

- Gemstones & Crystals:-
  - ➢ Cubic Zirconia
  - ➢ Zircon
  - ➢ Asphetic
  - ➢ Qabana Stone^^
  - ➢ White Topaz
  - ➢ White Spodumene
  - ➢ Opal
  - ➢ Triphane Gemstone^^

- ➤ White Beryl
- Secret Programmed Vastu Diviner^^ for West
- Specially Formulated Vastu Dosh Nivaran Yantra*^ for West
- Education Tower
- Naagmani Glowing^^
- Protection Bug Fossil^^^
- Antrikha / Space Stone / Space Stone Antrikha^^^
- Infinity Gem^^ (Faco Crystal) Green
- Rudrakshas:-
  - ➤ 1 Mukhi Trinetra Rudraksha^^
  - ➤ 1 Mukhi Jyotir Lingum Rudraksha^^
  - ➤ 2 Mukhi Rudraksha
  - ➤ 7 Mukhi Rudraksha
  - ➤ 16 Mukhi Rudraksha
  - ➤ 20 Mukhi Rudraksha
  - ➤ 25 Mukhi Rudraksha^^

Remedies for Study Room & Children's Room in South

- Gemstones & Crystals:-
  - ➤ Carnelian
  - ➤ Red Garnet
  - ➤ Qabana Stone^^
  - ➤ Red Jasper
  - ➤ Red Agate
  - ➤ Red Fluorite
  - ➤ Wolk Stone^^
  - ➤ Red Sapphire
  - ➤ Red Spinel
  - ➤ Red Coral
  - ➤ Heart Shaped Coral
- Secret Programmed Vastu Diviner^^ for West
- Specially Formulated Vastu Dosh Nivaran Yantra*^ for West

- Education Tower
- Naagmani Glowing^^
- Protection Bug Fossil^^^
- Antrikha / Space Stone / Space Stone Antrikha^^^
- Infinity Gem^^ (Faco Crystal) Green
- Rudrakshas:-
  - ➢ 1 Mukhi Rudraksha
  - ➢ 8 Mukhi Rudraksha
  - ➢ 17 Mukhi Rudraksha
  - ➢ 19 Mukhi Rudraksha^^
  - ➢ 26 Mukhi Rudraksha^^
  - ➢ 28 Mukhi Rudraksha^^

Remedies for Study Room & Children's Room in South-West

- Gemstones & Crystals:-
  - ➢ Smokey Quartz
  - ➢ Bronzite
  - ➢ Brown Agates
  - ➢ Grey Agates
  - ➢ Qabana Stone^^
  - ➢ Tiger's Eye Crystal
  - ➢ Amber
  - ➢ Wolk Stone^^
  - ➢ Smokey Topaz
  - ➢ Hessonite Garnet
  - ➢ Grey Japanese Coral
- Secret Programmed Vastu Diviner^^ for West
- Specially Formulated Vastu Dosh Nivaran Yantra*^ for West
- Education Tower
- Naagmani Glowing^^
- Protection Bug Fossil^^^
- Antrikha / Space Stone / Space Stone Antrikha^^^
- Infinity Gem^^ (Faco Crystal) Green

- Rudrakshas:-
  - 10 Mukhi Rudraksha
  - 11 Mukhi Rudraksha
  - 19 Mukhi Rudraksha
  - 28 Mukhi Rudraksha^^
  - 29 Mukhi Rudraksha^^
  - 1 Mukhi Trinetra Rudraksha^^
  - 1 Mukhi Jyotir Lingum Rudraksha^^
  - Charam Pashupati Nath Rudraksha^^^

Remedies for Study Room & Children's Room in West

- Gemstones & Crystals:-
  - Lapis Lazuli
  - Hematite
  - Angelite
  - Oyester Pearl^^
  - Moti Mani^^
  - Black Obsidian
  - Blue Tourmaline
  - Aquamarine
  - Blue Agate
  - Black Agate
  - Iolite
  - Conk Stone^^^
  - Sodalite
  - Blue Fluorite
  - Blue Amber
  - Azurite
  - Black Opal
  - Black Pearl
  - Black Onyx
  - Black Tourmalinc
  - Kyanite
  - Cordierite
  - Samudrik Stone^^

- ➢ Purple Sapphire
- ➢ Japanese Blue Coral
- ➢ Japanese Black Coral
- ➢ Black Spinel
- Secret Programmed Vastu Diviner^^ for West
- Specially Formulated Vastu Dosh Nivaran Yantra*^ for West
- Education Tower
- Naagmani Glowing^^
- Protection Bug Fossil^^^
- Antrikha / Space Stone / Space Stone Antrikha^^^
- Infinity Gem^^ (Faco Crystal) Green
- Rudraksha:-
  - ➢ 10 Mukhi Rudraksha
  - ➢ 11 Mukhi Rudraksha
  - ➢ 19 Mukhi Rudraksha
  - ➢ 28 Mukhi Rudraksha^^
  - ➢ 29 Mukhi Rudraksha^^
  - ➢ 1 Mukhi Trinetra Rudraksha^^
  - ➢ 1 Mukhi Jyotir Lingum Rudraksha^^

Remedies for Study Room & Children's Room in North-West

- White Gemstones & Crystals:-
  - ➢ Clear Quartz
  - ➢ White Agate
  - ➢ Adra Stone^^
  - ➢ White Jade
  - ➢ Fully Round Natural Pearl^
  - ➢ Mother of Pearl
  - ➢ Moonstone
  - ➢ Triphane Gemstone^^
- Secret Programmed Vastu Diviner^^ for West
- Specially Formulated Vastu Dosh Nivaran Yantra*^ for West

- Education Tower
- Naagmani Glowing^^
- Protection Bug Fossil^^^
- Antrikha / Space Stone / Space Stone Antrikha^^^
- Infinity Gem^^ (Faco Crystal) Green
- Rudraksha:-
  - ➢ 4 Mukhi Rudraksha
  - ➢ 13 Mukhi Rudraksha
  - ➢ 22 Mukhi Rudraksha^
  - ➢ 1 Mukhi Trinetra Rudraksha^^
  - ➢ 1 Mukhi Jyotir Lingum Rudraksha^^

Remedies for Study Room & Children's Room in North

- Gemstones & Crystals:-
  - ➢ Green Jade
  - ➢ Conk Stone^^^
  - ➢ Green Aventurine
  - ➢ Green Agate
  - ➢ Green Garnet
  - ➢ Green Tourmaline
  - ➢ Peridot
  - ➢ Hiddenite^
  - ➢ Green Amber
  - ➢ Green Turquoise
  - ➢ Malachite
  - ➢ Oyester Pearl^^
  - ➢ Moti Mani^^
  - ➢ Green Fluorite
  - ➢ Green Jasper
  - ➢ Amazonite
  - ➢ Florite
  - ➢ Samudrik Stone^^
  - ➢ Parasha Gemstone^^^
  - ➢ Green Tourmaline

  - ➢ Green Beryl^
- Secret Programmed Vastu Diviner^^ for West
- Specially Formulated Vastu Dosh Nivaran Yantra*^ for West
- Education Tower
- Naagmani Glowing^^
- Protection Bug Fossil^^^
- Antrikha / Space Stone / Space Stone Antrikha^^^
- Infinity Gem^^ (Faco Crystal) Green
- Rudraksha:-
  - ➢ 3 Mukhi Rudraksha
  - ➢ 6 Mukhi Rudraksha
  - ➢ 15 Mukhi Rudraksha
  - ➢ 21 Mukhi Rudraksha^
  - ➢ 25 Mukhi Rudraksha^^
  - ➢ 30 Mukhi Rudraksha^^

Remedies for Study Room & Children's Room in Bhrahmasthan

- Rudraksha:-
  - ➢ 1 Mukhi Rudraksha Gole Dana
  - ➢ 21 Mukhi Rudraksha
  - ➢ Combination of 16 Mukhi Rudraksha + 17 Mukhi Rudraksha + 18 Mukhi Rudraksha
  - ➢ Charam Pashupati Nath Rudraksha
    1 Mukhi Java Rudraksha^^
  - ➢ 1 Mukhi Java Rudraksha Gehuaan Dana^^
- Secret Programmed Vastu Diviner^^ for West
- Specially Formulated Vastu Dosh Nivaran Yantra*^ for West
- Education Tower
- Naagmani Glowing^^
- Protection Bug Fossil^^^
- Antrikha / Space Stone / Space Stone Antrikha^^^
- Infinity Gem^^ (Faco Crystal) Green

- Gemstones: Hiddenite, Parasha, Green Beryl, Green Florite, Yellow Florspar, Yellow Beryl, Yellow Spodumene, Scapolite, White Beryl

Remedies for Guest Room

In this section, we have provided the right vastu correction tools and vastu dosh nivaran products to be used to rectify ill effects of guest room in wrong directions.

Remedies for Guest Room in North-East

- 9 or 12 Yellow Pyramids
- Yellow Water Pyramid
- Pure Stone Pyramid
- Directional Healing Crystal for North-East
- Secret Programmed Vastu Diviner *^^ for North-East
- Specially Formulated Vastu Dosh Nivaran Yantra for North East *^
- Water Charging Crystals
- Negativity Cleaning Crystals
- Salt Lamp
- Indrajaal
- Protection Bug Fossil^^^

- Morogul Mani^
- Conk Pearl Gilabi Mani^^^
- Yellow Color
- Antrikha / Space Stone / Space Stone Antrikha*^^^
- Nav-Grah Pyramid Yantra
- Naagmani Glowing^^
- Kamakhya Sindhoor
- Sahastra Sampudh Mani^
- Parad Shivling
- Samudrik Mani^^
- Shwetark Ganpati
- Haldi ke Ganesh
- Kastoori

Remedies for Guest Room in East

- Directional Healing Crystal for East
- Secret Programmed Vastu Diviner^^ for East
- Specially Formulated Vastu Dosh Nivaran Yantra*^ for East
- Education Tower
- Morogul Mani^
- Pure Stone Pyramid
- 5 Orange Pyramids
- Orange Water Pyramid
- Sahastra Sampudh Mani^
- Water Charging Crystals
- Negativity Cleaning Crystals
- Salt Lamp
- Conk Pearl Gilabi Mani^^^
- Orange Color
- Infinity Gem^^ (Faco Crystal) Green
- Sher Ka Daant (Lions Teeth)

- Junglee Suar ka Daant (Wild Pig Teeth)

Remedies for Guest Room in South-East
- Directional Healing Crystal for South-East
- Secret Programmed Vastu Diviner*^^ for South-East
- Specially Formulated Vastu Dosh Nivaran Yantra*^ for South-East
- Deep Sea Corals *(Specific Patterns Needed)**
- Deep Sea Shells *(Specific Patterns Needed)**
- Pure & Natural Crystal Balls
- White Flowers
- Boar Pearl^^^
- Protection Bug Fossil^^^
- Negativity Cleaning Crystals
- Salt Lamp
- Bidaal Mani^^^
- Pure Stone Pyramid
- 7 Grey Pyramids
- 925 Sterling Silver Artifacts
- Silver & Sparkling White Colors
- Infinity Gem^^ (Faco Crystal) White
- Kaama Siyar Singhi
- Jungli Kaali Billi ki Jer*^^
- Kamakhaya Sindhoor

Remedies for Guest Room in South
- Directional Healing Crystal for South
- Secret Programmed Vastu Diviner^^ for South
- Specially Formulated Vastu Dosh Nivaran Yantra*^ for South
- Negativity Cleaning Crystals
- Salt Lamp

- Pure Stone Pyramid
- 8 Red Pyramids *
- Red Color
- Venu Mani^^^
- Raw Burmese Ruby
- Boar Pearl^^^
- Protection Bug Fossil^^^
- Red Lord Hanuman Photo / Idol
- Hatha Jodi Actual with Root
- Jungli Kaali Billi ki Jer*^^
- Kamakhaya Sindhoor
- Shwetark Ganpati
- Gaj Mukta^^^
- Jungli Suar ka Daant
- Dakshinavarti Shankh

Remedies for Guest Room in South-West

- Directional Healing Crystal for South-West
- Secret Programmed Vastu Diviner^^ for South-West
- Specially Formulated Vastu Dosh Nivaran Yantra*^ for South-West
- Negativity Cleaning Crystals
- Salt Lamp
- Pure Stone Pyramid
- 10 or 11 Brown Pyramids
- Rahu ki Kaudi
- Venu Mani^^^
- Brown & Grey Colors
- Naagmani Glowing^^
- Jungli Kaali Billi ki Jer⁺^^
- Hatha Jodi Jadh Samet (With Root)
- Brahmajaal

- Protection Bug Fossil^^^
- Boar Pearl^^^
- Parad Shivling
- Shwetark Ganpati
- Talismani Mani for Enemies
- Antrikha / Space Stone / Space Stone Antrikha^^^
- Sher ka Daant
- Shark Teeth
- Gaj Mukta^^^

Remedies for Guest Room in West

- Blue Water Pyramid
- Directional Healing Crystal for West
- Secret Programmed Vastu Diviner^^ for West
- Specially Formulated Vastu Dosh Nivaran Yantra*^ for West
- Pure Stone Pyramid
- 10 or 11 Black / Blue Pyramids
- Water Charging Crystals
- Negativity Cleaning Crystals
- Salt Lamp
- Morogul Mani^
- Conk Pearl Gilabi Mani^^^
- Education Tower
- Raw Sugilite Crystal
- Raw Turquoise Crystals
- Black & Blue Colors
- Infinity Gem^^ (Faco Crystal) Green
- Narmadeshwar Shivling Black
- Saam Siyar Singhi
- Jungli Kaali Billi ki Jer*^^
- Hatha Jodi
- Gaj Mukta^^^

- Dakshinavarti Shankh
- Sahastra Sampudh Mani^
- Dhan ka Bandha^
- Samudrik Mani^^

Remedies for Guest Room in North

- Green Water Pyramid
- Directional Healing Crystal for North
- Secret Programmed Vastu Diviner^^ for North
- Specially Formulated Vastu Dosh Nivaran Yantra*^ for North
- Water Charging Crystals
- Negativity Cleaning Crystals
- Salt Lamp
- Pure Stone Pyramid
- 3 or 6 Green Pyramids
- Money Eggs^^
- Infinity Gem^^ (Faco Crystal) Green
- Morogul Mani^
- Green Color
- Plants
- Samudrik Mani^^
- Raw Emerald
- Conk Pearl Gilabi Mani^^^
- Indrajaal, Brahmajaal
- Jungli Kaali Billi ki Jer*^^
- Hatha Jodi with Actual Root
- Saam Siyar Singhi
- Sahastra Sampudh Mani^
- Dakshinavarti Shankh
- Dhan ka Bandha*^
- Asphetic Shri Yantra

Remedies for Guest Room in Bhrahmasthan

- Secret Programmed Vastu Diviner^^ for Brahmasthaan
- Specially Formulated Vastu Dosh Nivaran Yantra^^ for Brahmasthaan
- Kale Ghodhe ki Naal
- Nav-Grah Pyramid Yantra
- Antrikha / Space Stone / Space Stone Antrikha^^^
- Infinity Gem^^ (Faco Crystal) White & Green
- Vishnu Chakra Moti^^
- Combination of 20-140 Vastu Items & Products
- Fully Round Natural Pearl^^
- Tutmak Stone^^
- Timi Stone^^^
- Adra Stone^^
- Enemy Stone^^
- **Conk Stone^^^**
- Qabana Stone^^^
- Protection Bug Fossil^^^
- Eagle Stone^^^
- Triphane Gemstone ^^
- Cordierite^^
- Nagmani Black^
- Naagmani Glowing^^^
- Combination of Brahmajaal + Indrajaal
- Combination of Kaali Billi ki Jer + Siyar Singhi + Mota Hatha Jodi
- Kamakhaya Sindoor
- Parad Shivling
- Deep Sea Corals^
- Deep Sea Shells^
- Money Eggs^^
- Combination of 120-140 Vastu Healing Products
- Kastoori
- Asphetic Shri Yantra

- Dhan ka Bandha*^
- Moon Rock^^
- Natural Pearl Blisters

Remedies for Drawing Room & Dining Room

In this section, we have provided the right vastu correction tools and vastu dosh nivaran products to be used to rectify ill effects of drawing room and dining room in wrong directions.

Remedies for Drawing Room & Dining Room in South-East

- Gemstones & Crystals:-
  - Cubic Zirconia
  - Zircon
  - Asphetic
  - Qabana Stone^^
  - White Topaz
  - White Spodumene
  - Opal
  - Triphane Gemstone^^
  - White Beryl
- Rudrakshas:-

> ➤ 1 Mukhi Trinetra Rudraksha^^
> ➤ 1 Mukhi Jyotir Lingum Rudraksha^^
> ➤ 2 Mukhi Rudraksha
> ➤ 7 Mukhi Rudraksha
> ➤ 16 Mukhi Rudraksha
> ➤ 20 Mukhi Rudraksha
> ➤ 25 Mukhi Rudraksha^^

Remedies for Drawing Room & Dining Room in South

- Gemstones & Crystals:-
  - ➤ Carnelian
  - ➤ Red Garnet
  - ➤ Qabana Stone^^
  - ➤ Red Jasper
  - ➤ Red Agate
  - ➤ Red Fluorite
  - ➤ Wolk Stone^^
  - ➤ Red Sapphire
  - ➤ Red Spinel
  - ➤ Red Coral
  - ➤ Heart Shaped Coral
- Rudrakshas:-
  - ➤ 1 Mukhi Rudraksha
  - ➤ 8 Mukhi Rudraksha
  - ➤ 17 Mukhi Rudraksha
  - ➤ 19 Mukhi Rudraksha^^
  - ➤ 26 Mukhi Rudraksha^^
  - ➤ 28 Mukhi Rudraksha^^

Remedies for Drawing Room & Dining Room in South-West

- Gemstones & Crystals:-
  - ➤ Smokey Quartz
  - ➤ Bronzite

151

- ➤ Brown Agates
- ➤ Grey Agates
- ➤ Qabana Stone^^
- ➤ Tiger's Eye Crystal
- ➤ Amber
- ➤ Wolk Stone^^
- ➤ Smokey Topaz
- ➤ Hessonite Garnet
- ➤ Grey Japanese Coral
- Rudrakshas:-
  - ➤ 10 Mukhi Rudraksha
  - ➤ 11 Mukhi Rudraksha
  - ➤ 19 Mukhi Rudraksha
  - ➤ 28 Mukhi Rudraksha^^
  - ➤ 29 Mukhi Rudraksha^^
  - ➤ 1 Mukhi Trinetra Rudraksha^^
  - ➤ 1 Mukhi Jyotir Lingum Rudraksha^^
  - ➤ Charam Pashupati Nath Rudraksha^^^

Remedies for Drawing Room & Dining Room in North-West

- White Gemstones & Crystals:-
  - ➤ Clear Quartz
  - ➤ White Agate
  - ➤ Adra Stone^^
  - ➤ White Jade
  - ➤ Fully Round Natural Pearl^
  - ➤ Mother of Pearl
  - ➤ Moonstone
  - ➤ Triphane Gemstone^^
- Rudraksha:-
  - ➤ 4 Mukhi Rudraksha
  - ➤ 13 Mukhi Rudraksha
  - ➤ 22 Mukhi Rudraksha^
  - ➤ 1 Mukhi Trinetra Rudraksha^^
  - ➤ 1 Mukhi Jyotir Lingum Rudraksha^^

Remedies for Garage

In this section, we have provided the right vastu correction tools and vastu dosh nivaran products to be used to rectify ill effects of garage and car parking space in wrong directions.

Remedies for Garage in North-East

- 9 or 12 Yellow Pyramids
- Yellow Water Pyramid
- Pure Stone Pyramid
- Directional Healing Crystal for North-East
- Secret Programmed Vastu Diviner *^^ for North-East
- Specially Formulated Vastu Dosh Nivaran Yantra for North East *^

Remedies for Garage in East
- Directional Healing Crystal for East
- Secret Programmed Vastu Diviner^^ for East
- Specially Formulated Vastu Dosh Nivaran Yantra*^ for East

Remedies for Garage in South
- Directional Healing Crystal for South
- Secret Programmed Vastu Diviner^^ for South
- Specially Formulated Vastu Dosh Nivaran Yantra*^ for South
- Negativity Cleaning Crystals
- Salt Lamp
- Pure Stone Pyramid
- 8 Red Pyramids *
- Red Color

Remedies for Garage in South-West
- Directional Healing Crystal for South-West
- Secret Programmed Vastu Diviner^^ for South-West
- Specially Formulated Vastu Dosh Nivaran Yantra*^ for South-West
- Negativity Cleaning Crystals
- Salt Lamp
- Pure Stone Pyramid
- 10 or 11 Brown Pyramids
- Rahu ki Kaudi

Remedies for Garage in West
- Blue Water Pyramid
- Directional Healing Crystal for West

- Secret Programmed Vastu Diviner^^ for West
- Specially Formulated Vastu Dosh Nivaran Yantra*^ for West
- Pure Stone Pyramid
- 10 or 11 Black / Blue Pyramids
- Water Charging Crystals
- Negativity Cleaning Crystals
- Salt Lamp

Remedies for Garage in North
- Green Water Pyramid
- Directional Healing Crystal for North
- Secret Programmed Vastu Diviner^^ for North
- Specially Formulated Vastu Dosh Nivaran Yantra*^ for North
- Water Charging Crystals
- Negativity Cleaning Crystals
- Salt Lamp
- Pure Stone Pyramid
- 3 or 6 Green Pyramids

Remedies for Basement

In this section, we have provided the right vastu correction tools and vastu dosh nivaran products to be used to rectify ill effects of basement in wrong directions.

Remedies for Basement in Bhrahmasthan

- Secret Programmed Vastu Diviner^^ for Brahmasthaan
- Specially Formulated Vastu Dosh Nivaran Yantra^^ for Brahmasthaan
- Kale Ghodhe ki Naal
- Nav-Grah Pyramid Yantra
- Antrikha / Space Stone / Space Stone Antrikha^^^
- Vishnu Chakra Moti^^
- Combination of 20-140 Vastu Items & Products
- Fully Round Natural Pearl^^
- Tutmak Stone^^
- Timi Stone^^^
- Adra Stone^^

- Enemy Stone^^
- **Conk Stone^^^**
- Qabana Stone^^^
- Protection Bug Fossil^^^
- Eagle Stone^^^
- Triphane Gemstone ^^
- Cordierite^^
- Nagmani Black^
- Naagmani Glowing^^^
- Combination of Brahmajaal + Indrajaal
- Combination of Kaali Billi ki Jer + Siyar Singhi + Mota Hatha Jodi
- Kamakhaya Sindoor
- Parad Shivling
- Deep Sea Corals^
- Deep Sea Shells^
- Money Eggs^^
- Combination of 120-140 Vastu Healing Products
- Kastoori
- Asphetic Shri Yantra
- Dhan ka Bandha*^
- Moon Rock^^
- Natural Pearl Blisters
- Rudraksha:-
  - 1 Mukhi Rudraksha Gole Dana
  - 21 Mukhi Rudraksha
  - Combination of 16 Mukhi Rudraksha + 17 Mukhi Rudraksha + 18 Mukhi Rudraksha
  - Charam Pashupati Nath Rudraksha 1 Mukhi Java Rudraksha^^
  - 1 Mukhi Java Rudraksha Gehuaan Dana^^
- Gemstones: Hiddenite, Parasha, Green Beryl, Green Florite, Yellow Florspar, Yellow Beryl, Yellow Spodumene, Scapolite, White Beryl

Remedies for Basement in South

- Directional Healing Crystal for South
- Secret Programmed Vastu Diviner^^ for South
- Specially Formulated Vastu Dosh Nivaran Yantra*^ for South
- Negativity Cleaning Crystals
- Salt Lamp
- Pure Stone Pyramid
- 8 Red Pyramids *
- Red Color
- Venu Mani^^^
- Raw Burmese Ruby
- Boar Pearl^^^
- Protection Bug Fossil^^^
- Red Lord Hanuman Photo / Idol
- Hatha Jodi Actual with Root
- Jungli Kaali Billi ki Jer*^^
- Kamakhaya Sindhoor
- Shwetark Ganpati
- Gaj Mukta^^^
- Jungli Suar ka Daant
- Dakshinavarti Shankh
- Red Gemstones & Crystals:-
  - Carnelian
  - Red Garnet
  - Qabana Stone^^
  - Red Jasper
  - Red Agate
  - Red Fluorite
  - Wolk Stone^^
  - Red Sapphire
  - Red Spinel
  - Red Coral
  - Heart Shaped Coral

- Rudrakshas:-
  - ➢ 1 Mukhi Rudraksha
  - ➢ 8 Mukhi Rudraksha
  - ➢ 17 Mukhi Rudraksha
  - ➢ 19 Mukhi Rudraksha^^
  - ➢ 26 Mukhi Rudraksha^^
  - ➢ 28 Mukhi Rudraksha^^

Remedies for Basement in South-West

- Directional Healing Crystal for South-West
- Secret Programmed Vastu Diviner^^ for South-West
- Specially Formulated Vastu Dosh Nivaran Yantra*^ for South-West
- Negativity Cleaning Crystals
- Salt Lamp
- Pure Stone Pyramid
- 10 or 11 Brown Pyramids
- Rahu ki Kaudi
- Venu Mani^^^
- Brown & Grey Colors
- Naagmani Glowing^^
- Jungli Kaali Billi ki Jer*^^
- Hatha Jodi Jadh Samet (With Root)
- Brahmajaal
- Protection Bug Fossil^^^
- Boar Pearl^^^
- Parad Shivling
- Shwetark Ganpati
- Talismani Mani for Enemies
- Antrikha / Space Stone / Space Stone Antrikha^^^
- Sher ka Daant
- Shark Teeth
- Gaj Mukta^^^

- Gemstones & Crystals:-
  - Smokey Quartz
  - Bronzite
  - Brown Agates
  - Grey Agates
  - Qabana Stone^^
  - Tiger's Eye Crystal
  - Amber
  - Wolk Stone^^
  - Smokey Topaz
  - Hessonite Garnet
  - Grey Japanese Coral
- Rudrakshas:-
  - 10 Mukhi Rudraksha
  - 11 Mukhi Rudraksha
  - 19 Mukhi Rudraksha
  - 28 Mukhi Rudraksha^^
  - 29 Mukhi Rudraksha^^
  - 1 Mukhi Trinetra Rudraksha^^
  - 1 Mukhi Jyotir Lingum Rudraksha^^
  - Charam Pashupati Nath Rudraksha^^^

Remedies for Basement in West
- Blue Water Pyramid
- Directional Healing Crystal for West
- Secret Programmed Vastu Diviner^^ for West
- Specially Formulated Vastu Dosh Nivaran Yantra*^ for West
- Pure Stone Pyramid
- 10 or 11 Black / Blue Pyramids
- Water Charging Crystals
- Negativity Cleaning Crystals
- Salt Lamp
- Morogul Mani^
- Conk Pearl Gilabi Mani^^^

- Education Tower
- Raw Sugilite Crystal
- Raw Turquoise Crystals
- Black & Blue Colors
- Narmadeshwar Shivling Black
- Saam Siyar Singhi
- Jungli Kaali Billi ki Jer*^^
- Hatha Jodi
- Gaj Mukta^^^
- Dakshinavarti Shankh
- Sahastra Sampudh Mani^
- Dhan ka Bandha^
- Samudrik Mani^^
- Gemstones & Crystals:-
  - Lapis Lazuli
  - Hematite
  - Angelite
  - Oyester Pearl^^
  - Moti Mani^^
  - Black Obsidian
  - Blue Tourmaline
  - Aquamarine
  - Blue Agate
  - Black Agate
  - Iolite
  - Conk Stone^^^
  - Sodalite
  - Blue Fluorite
  - Blue Amber
  - Azurite
  - Black Opal
  - Black Pearl
  - Black Onyx
  - Black Tourmaline
  - Kyanite
  - Cordierite

- ➢ Samudrik Stone^^
- ➢ Purple Sapphire
- ➢ Japanese Blue Coral
- ➢ Japanese Black Coral
- ➢ Black Spinel
- Rudraksha:-
  - ➢ 10 Mukhi Rudraksha
  - ➢ 11 Mukhi Rudraksha
  - ➢ 19 Mukhi Rudraksha
  - ➢ 28 Mukhi Rudraksha^^
  - ➢ 29 Mukhi Rudraksha^^
  - ➢ 1 Mukhi Trinetra Rudraksha^^
  - ➢ 1 Mukhi Jyotir Lingum Rudraksha^^

Remedies for Basement in North-West

- Directional Healing Crystal for North-West
- Secret Programmed Vastu Diviner^^ for North-West
- Negativity Cleaning Crystals
- Salt Lamp
- Megha Mani^^
- Pure Stone Pyramid
- 4 White Pyramids
- Moon Rock^
- Aakash Mani Nubh Mani^^
- Pearl White Color
- Narmadeshwar Shivling White
- Pearl Blisters
- Protection Bug Fossil^^^
- Bidaal Mani^^^
- Siyar Singhi Joda Male Female Pair
- White Gemstones & Crystals:-
  - ➢ Clear Quartz
  - ➢ White Agate
  - ➢ Adra Stone^^

- ➢ White Jade
- ➢ Fully Round Natural Pearl^
- ➢ Mother of Pearl
- ➢ Moonstone
- ➢ Triphane Gemstone^^
- Rudraksha:-
  - ➢ 4 Mukhi Rudraksha
  - ➢ 13 Mukhi Rudraksha
  - ➢ 22 Mukhi Rudraksha^
  - ➢ 1 Mukhi Trinetra Rudraksha^^
  - ➢ 1 Mukhi Jyotir Lingum Rudraksha^^

Remedies for Basement in South-East

- Directional Healing Crystal for South-East
- Secret Programmed Vastu Diviner*^^ for South-East
- Specially Formulated Vastu Dosh Nivaran Yantra*^ for South-East
- Deep Sea Corals (*Specific Patterns Needed*)*
- Deep Sea Shells (*Specific Patterns Needed*)*
- Pure & Natural Crystal Balls
- White Flowers
- Boar Pearl^^^
- Protection Bug Fossil^^^
- Negativity Cleaning Crystals
- Salt Lamp
- Bidaal Mani^^^
- Pure Stone Pyramid
- 7 Grey Pyramids
- 925 Sterling Silver Artifacts
- Silver & Sparkling White Colors
- Kaama Siyar Singhi
- Jungli Kaali Billi ki Jer*^^
- Kamakhaya Sindhoor
- Gemstones & Crystals:-

- ➢ Cubic Zirconia
- ➢ Zircon
- ➢ Asphetic
- ➢ Qabana Stone^^
- ➢ White Topaz
- ➢ White Spodumene
- ➢ Opal
- ➢ Triphane Gemstone^^
- ➢ White Beryl
- Rudrakshas:-
  - ➢ 1 Mukhi Trinetra Rudraksha^^
  - ➢ 1 Mukhi Jyotir Lingum Rudraksha^^
  - ➢ 2 Mukhi Rudraksha
  - ➢ 7 Mukhi Rudraksha
  - ➢ 16 Mukhi Rudraksha
  - ➢ 20 Mukhi Rudraksha
  - ➢ 25 Mukhi Rudraksha^^

Remedies for Verandah

In this section, we have provided the right vastu correction tools and vastu dosh nivaran products to be used to rectify ill effects of verandah in wrong directions.

Remedies for Verandah in South-East

- Directional Healing Crystal for South-East
- Secret Programmed Vastu Diviner*^^ for South-East
- Specially Formulated Vastu Dosh Nivaran Yantra*^ for South-East
- Deep Sea Corals *(Specific Patterns Needed)*
- Deep Sea Shells *(Specific Patterns Needed)*
- Pure & Natural Crystal Balls
- White Flowers
- Boar Pearl^^^
- Protection Bug Fossil^^^
- Negativity Cleaning Crystals
- Salt Lamp

- Bidaal Mani^^^
- Pure Stone Pyramid
- 7 Grey Pyramids
- 925 Sterling Silver Artifacts
- Silver & Sparkling White Colors
- Kaama Siyar Singhi
- Jungli Kaali Billi ki Jer*^^
- Kamakhaya Sindhoor

Remedies for Verandah in South

- Directional Healing Crystal for South
- Secret Programmed Vastu Diviner^^ for South
- Specially Formulated Vastu Dosh Nivaran Yantra*^ for South
- Negativity Cleaning Crystals
- Salt Lamp
- Pure Stone Pyramid
- 8 Red Pyramids *
- Red Color
- Venu Mani^^^
- Raw Burmese Ruby
- Boar Pearl^^^
- Protection Bug Fossil^^^
- Red Lord Hanuman Photo / Idol
- Hatha Jodi Actual with Root
- Jungli Kaali Billi ki Jer*^^
- Kamakhaya Sindhoor
- Shwetark Ganpati
- Gaj Mukta^^^
- Jungli Suar ka Daant
- Dakshinavarti Shankh

Remedies for Verandah in South-West

- Directional Healing Crystal for South-West
- Secret Programmed Vastu Diviner^^ for South-West
- Specially Formulated Vastu Dosh Nivaran Yantra*^ for South-West
- Negativity Cleaning Crystals
- Salt Lamp
- Pure Stone Pyramid
- 10 or 11 Brown Pyramids
- Rahu ki Kaudi
- Venu Mani^^^
- Brown & Grey Colors
- Naagmani Glowing^^
- Jungli Kaali Billi ki Jer*^^
- Hatha Jodi Jadh Samet (With Root)
- Brahmajaal
- Protection Bug Fossil^^^
- Boar Pearl^^^
- Parad Shivling
- Shwetark Ganpati
- Talismani Mani for Enemies
- Antrikha / Space Stone / Space Stone Antrikha^^^
- Sher ka Daant
- Shark Teeth
- Gaj Mukta^^^

Remedies for Verandah in West

- Directional Healing Crystal for North-West
- Secret Programmed Vastu Diviner^^ for North-West
- Negativity Cleaning Crystals
- Salt Lamp
- Megha Mani^^

- Pure Stone Pyramid
- 4 White Pyramids
- Moon Rock^
- Aakash Mani Nubh Mani^^
- Infinity Gem^^ (Faco Crystal) White
- Pearl White Color
- Narmadeshwar Shivling White
- Pearl Blisters
- Protection Bug Fossil^^^
- Bidaal Mani^^^
- Siyar Singhi Joda Male Female Pair

Remedies for Verandah in North-West

- Directional Healing Crystal for North-West
- Secret Programmed Vastu Diviner^^ for North-West
- Negativity Cleaning Crystals
- Salt Lamp
- Megha Mani^^
- Pure Stone Pyramid
- 4 White Pyramids
- Moon Rock^
- Aakash Mani Nubh Mani^^
- Pearl White Color
- Narmadeshwar Shivling White
- Pearl Blisters
- Protection Bug Fossil^^^
- Bidaal Mani^^^
- Siyar Singhi Joda Male Female Pair

Remedies for Office, Director / Boss / CEO / Founder's Cabin or Room

In this section, we have provided the right vastu correction tools and vastu dosh nivaran products to be used to rectify ill effects of office, director boss ceo founder's cabin or room in wrong directions.

Remedies for Office, Director / Boss / CEO / Founder's Cabin or Room in North East

- 9 or 12 Yellow Pyramids
- Yellow Water Pyramid
- Pure Stone Pyramid
- Directional Healing Crystal for North-East
- Secret Programmed Vastu Diviner *^^ for North East
- Specially Formulated Vastu Dosh Nivaran Yantra for North East *^

169

- Water Charging Crystals
- Negativity Cleaning Crystals
- Salt Lamp
- Indrajaal
- Protection Bug Fossil^^^
- Morogul Mani^
- Conk Pearl Gilabi Mani^^^
- Yellow Color
- Antrikha / Space Stone / Space Stone Antrikha*^^^
- Nav-Grah Pyramid Yantra
- Naagmani Glowing^^
- Kamakhya Sindhoor
- Sahastra Sampudh Mani^
- Parad Shivling
- Samudrik Mani^^
- Shwetark Ganpati
- Haldi ke Ganesh
- Kastoori
- Gems & Crystals:-
  - Yellow Jade
  - Yellow Aventurine
  - Yellow Jasper
  - Yellow Garnet
  - Conk Stone^^^
  - Deep Yellow Citrine
  - Yellow Triphane Gemstone^^
  - Yellow Tourmaline
  - Yellow Topaz
  - Yellow Opal
  - Oyester Pearl^^
  - Moti Mani^^
  - Yellow Labradorite
  - Yellow Agate
  - Yellow Florspar
  - Yellow Spodumene

- ➤ Yellow Beryl
- ➤ Scapolite
- ➤ Samudrik Stone^^
- ➤ Golden Yellow Japanese Coral

Remedies for Office, Director / Boss / CEO / Founder's Cabin or Room in East

- Directional Healing Crystal for East
- Secret Programmed Vastu Diviner^^ for East
- Specially Formulated Vastu Dosh Nivaran Yantra*^ for East
- Education Tower
- Morogul Mani^
- Pure Stone Pyramid
- 5 Orange Pyramids
- Orange Water Pyramid
- Sahastra Sampudh Mani^
- Water Charging Crystals
- Negativity Cleaning Crystals
- Salt Lamp
- Conk Pearl Gilabi Mani^^^
- Orange Color
- Infinity Gem^^ (Faco Crystal) Green
- Sher Ka Daant (Lions Teeth)
- Junglee Suar ka Daant (Wild Pig Teeth)
- Gems & Crystals:-
  - ➤ Orange Sunstone
  - ➤ Orange Topaz
  - ➤ Orange Tourmaline
  - ➤ Orange Garnet
  - ➤ Orange Opal
  - ➤ Conk Stone^^^
  - ➤ Orange Sphalerite
  - ➤ Orange Flourite
  - ➤ Carnelian

➤ Oyester Pearl^^
➤ Moti Mani^^
➤ Orange Agate
➤ Peach Aventurine
➤ Orange Beryl
➤ Orange Citrine
➤ Samudrik Stone^^
➤ Amber

Remedies for Office, Director / Boss / CEO / Founder's Cabin or Room in South-East

- Directional Healing Crystal for South-East
- Secret Programmed Vastu Diviner*^^ for South-East
- Specially Formulated Vastu Dosh Nivaran Yantra*^ for South-East
- Deep Sea Corals (Specific Patterns Needed)*
- Deep Sea Shells (Specific Patterns Needed)*
- Pure & Natural Crystal Balls
- White Flowers
- Boar Pearl^^^
- Protection Bug Fossil^^^
- Negativity Cleaning Crystals
- Salt Lamp
- Bidaal Mani^^^
- Pure Stone Pyramid
- 7 Grey Pyramids
- 925 Sterling Silver Artifacts
- Silver & Sparkling White Colors
- Infinity Gem^^ (Faco Crystal) Green
- Kaama Siyar Singhi
- Jungli Kaali Billi ki Jer*^^
- Kamakhaya Sindhoor
- Gemstones & Crystals:-

- ➤ Cubic Zirconia
- ➤ Zircon
- ➤ Asphetic
- ➤ Qabana Stone^^
- ➤ White Topaz
- ➤ White Spodumene
- ➤ Opal
- ➤ Triphanc Gemstone^^
- ➤ White Beryl

Remedies for Office, Director / Boss / CEO / Founder's Cabin or Room in North-West

- Directional Healing Crystal for North-West
- Secret Programmed Vastu Diviner^^ for North-West
- Negativity Cleaning Crystals
- Salt Lamp
- Megha Mani^^
- Pure Stone Pyramid
- 4 White Pyramids
- Moon Rock^
- Aakash Mani Nubh Mani^^
- Infinity Gem^^ (Faco Crystal) White
- Pearl White Color
- Narmadeshwar Shivling White
- Pearl Blisters
- Protection Bug Fossil^^^
- Bidaal Mani^^^
- Siyar Singhi Joda Male Female Pair
- White Gemstones & Crystals:-
  - ➤ Clear Quartz
  - ➤ White Agate
  - ➤ Adra Stone^^
  - ➤ White Jade
  - ➤ Fully Round Natural Pearl^

- ➢ Mother of Pearl
- ➢ Moonstone
- ➢ Triphane Gemstone^^

Remedies for Office, Director / Boss / CEO / Founder's Cabin or Room in Brahmasthaan

- Secret Programmed Vastu Diviner^^ for Brahmasthaan
- Specially Formulated Vastu Dosh Nivaran Yantra^^ for Brahmasthaan
- Kale Ghodhe ki Naal
- Nav-Grah Pyramid Yantra
- Antrikha / Space Stone / Space Stone Antrikha^^^
- Infinity Gem^^ (Faco Crystal) White & Green
- Vishnu Chakra Moti^^
- Combination of 20-140 Vastu Items & Products
- Fully Round Natural Pearl^^
- Tutmak Stone^^
- Timi Stone^^^
- Adra Stone^^
- Enemy Stone^^
- **Conk Stone^^^**
- Qabana Stone^^^
- Protection Bug Fossil^^^
- Eagle Stone^^^
- Triphane Gemstone ^^
- Cordierite^^
- Nagmani Black^
- Naagmani Glowing^^^
- Combination of Brahmajaal + Indrajaal
- Combination of Kaali Billi ki Jer + Siyar Singhi + Mota Hatha Jodi
- Kamakhaya Sindoor
- Parad Shivling

- Deep Sea Corals^
- Deep Sea Shells^
- Money Eggs^^
- Combination of 120-140 Vastu Healing Products
- Kastoori
- Asphetic Shri Yantra
- Dhan ka Bandha*^
- Moon Rock^^
- Natural Pearl Blisters
- Rudraksha:-
  - ➢ 1 Mukhi Rudraksha Gole Dana
  - ➢ 21 Mukhi Rudraksha
  - ➢ Combination of 16 Mukhi Rudraksha + 17 Mukhi Rudraksha + 18 Mukhi Rudraksha
  - ➢ Charam Pashupati Nath Rudraksha 1 Mukhi Java Rudraksha^^
  - ➢ 1 Mukhi Java Rudraksha Gehuaan Dana^^
- Gemstones: Hiddenite, Parasha, Green Beryl, Green Florite, Yellow Florspar, Yellow Beryl, Yellow Spodumene, Scapolite, White Beryl

Remedies for <u>Entrance</u> of the Office, Director / Boss / CEO / Founder's Cabin or Room

- Ganesh Ji Inside & Outside*
- Pakua Mirror Outside*
- Vastu Dosh Nivaran Rudraksha Yantra*^
- Antrikha / Space Stone / Space Stone Antrikha*^^
- Kale Ghodhe ki Naal^
- Secret Programmed Vastu Diviner with Gold Line*^^^ for Entrance
- Specially Formulated Vastu Dosh Nivaran Yantra for Brahmasthaan*^
- Protection Bug Fossil^^^
- Morogul Mani^
- Conk Pearl Gilabi Mani^^^

- Naagmani Glowing^^
- Sahastra Sampudh Mani^
- Samudrik Mani^^
- Haldi ke Ganesh
- Kastoori

Remedies for Shops & Showrooms

In this section, we have provided the right vastu correction tools and vastu dosh nivaran products to be used to rectify ill effects of shops and showrooms in wrong directions.

Vastu Remedies For High Money Inflow, Monetory Gains, Higher Profit Margins

- Morogul Mani^
- Conk Pearl Gilabi Mani^^^
- Antrikha / Space Stone / Space Stone Antrikha*^^^
- Naagmani Glowing^^
- Kamakhya Sindhoor
- Sahastra Sampudh Mani^
- Parad Shivling
- Samudrik Mani^^
- Kastoori
- Secret Programmed Vastu Diviner^^ for North
- Specially Formulated Vastu Dosh Nivaran Yantra*^ for North
- 3 or 6 Green Pyramids

- Money Eggs^^
- Infinity Gem^^ (Faco Crystal) Green
- Green & Off White Color
- Green Plants
- Raw Emerald
- Dakshinavarti Shankh
- Dhan ka Bandha*^
- Asphetic Shri Yantra
- Jungli Kaali Billi ki Jer*^^
- Hatha Jodi with Actual Root
- Saam Siyar Singhi

Vastu Remedies For Good Clientale, High Foot-Fall, Large Intake of Customers & Clients, Higher Number of Orders & Good Reputation

- Secret Programmed Vastu Diviner^^ for West
- Specially Formulated Vastu Dosh Nivaran Yantra*^ for West
- Secret Programmed Vastu Diviner*^^ for South-East
- Specially Formulated Vastu Dosh Nivaran Yantra*^ for South-East
- Deep Sea Corals (Specific Patterns Needed)*
- Deep Sea Shells (Specific Patterns Needed)*
- 10 or 11 Black / Blue Pyramids
- Water Charging Crystals
- Negativity Cleaning Crystals
- Morogul Mani^
- Conk Pearl Gilabi Mani^^^
- Raw Sugilite Crystal
- Raw Turquoise Crystals
- Black & Blue Colors
- Infinity Gem^^ (Faco Crystal) Green & White
- Narmadeshwar Shivling Black

- Saam Siyar Singhi
- Jungli Kaali Billi ki Jer*^^
- Hatha Jodi
- Protection Bug Fossil^^^
- Bidaal Mani^^^
- Kamakhaya Sindhoor
- Gaj Mukta^^^
- Dakshinavarti Shankh
- Sahastra Sampudh Mani^
- Dhan ka Bandha^
- Samudrik Mani^^
- Boar Pearl^^^

Vastu Remedies For Good Administration & Management, Business Expansion, Long Term Stability & Loyal Workforce

- Secret Programmed Vastu Diviner^^ for South
- Specially Formulated Vastu Dosh Nivaran Yantra*^ for South
- Directional Healing Crystal for South-West
- Secret Programmed Vastu Diviner^^ for South-West
- Specially Formulated Vastu Dosh Nivaran Yantra*^ for South-West
- Red & Brown Color
- Venu Mani^^^
- Raw Burmese Ruby
- Boar Pearl^^^
- Hatha Jodi Actual with Root
- Jungli Kaali Billi ki Jer*^^
- Kamakhaya Sindhoor
- Gaj Mukta^^^
- Jungli Suar ka Daant
- Dakshinavarti Shankh

- Rahu ki Kaudi
- Naagmani Glowing^^
- Protection Bug Fossil^^^
- Boar Pearl^^^
- Parad Shivling
- Shwetark Ganpati
- Sher ka Daant
- Shark Teeth
- Gaj Mukta^^^
- Talismani Mani for Enemies
- Antrikha / Space Stone / Space Stone Antrikha^^^

Vastu Remedies For Wrong Entrance of Shops or Showrooms

- Ganesh Ji Inside & Outside*
- Pakua Mirror Outside*
- Vastu Dosh Nivaran Rudraksha Yantra*^
- Antrikha / Space Stone / Space Stone Antrikha*^^
- Kale Ghodhe ki Naal^
- Secret Programmed Vastu Diviner with Gold Line*^^^ for Entrance
- Specially Formulated Vastu Dosh Nivaran Yantra for Brahmasthaan*^
- Protection Bug Fossil^^^
- Morogul Mani^
- Conk Pearl Gilabi Mani^^^
- Naagmani Glowing^^
- Sahastra Sampudh Mani^
- Samudrik Mani^^
- Haldi ke Ganesh
- Kastoori

Remedies of Cash Box, Galla, Safe & Locker

In this section, we have provided the right vastu correction tools and vastu dosh nivaran products to be used to rectify ill effects of cash box, galla, safe and locker in wrong directions.

Remedies of Cash Box, Locker, Safe in North-East

(Place these Remedies inside the Cash Box or Locker in its North)

- Secret Programmed Vastu Diviner *^^ for North-East
- Protection Bug Fossil^^^
- Morogul Mani^
- Conk Pearl Gilabi Mani^^^
- Antrikha / Space Stone / Space Stone Antrikha*^^^
- Naagmani Glowing^^
- Sahastra Sampudh Mani^
- Samudrik Mani^^
- Money Eggs
- Infinity Gem (Faco Crystal) Green
- Kaali Billi ki Jer^^^
- Saam Siyar Singhi
- Dakshinavarti Shankh
- Dhan ka Bandha^^^

Remedies of Cash Box, Locker, Safe in East

- Secret Programmed Vastu Diviner^^ for East
- Morogul Mani^
- Sahastra Sampudh Mani^
- Conk Pearl Gilabi Mani^^^
- Infinity Gem^^ (Faco Crystal) Green

- Sher Ka Daant (Lions Teeth)
- Junglee Suar ka Daant (Wild Pig Teeth)
- Gems & Crystals:-
  - Conk Stone^^^
  - Oyester Pearl^^
  - Moti Mani^^
  - Samudrik Stone^^

Remedies of Cash Box, Locker, Safe in South-East

- Secret Programmed Vastu Diviner*^^ for South-East
- Deep Sea Corals *(Specific Patterns Needed)**
- Deep Sea Shells *(Specific Patterns Needed)**
- Boar Pearl^^^
- Protection Bug Fossil^^^
- Bidaal Mani^^^
- Infinity Gem^^ (Faco Crystal) White
- Jungli Kaali Billi ki Jer*^^
- Gemstones & Crystals:-
  - Qabana Stone^^
  - Triphane Gemstone^^
- Rudrakshas:-
  - 1 Mukhi Trinetra Rudraksha^^
  - 1 Mukhi Jyotir Lingum Rudraksha^^
  - 25 Mukhi Rudraksha^^

Remedies of Cash Box, Locker, Safe in South

- Secret Programmed Vastu Diviner^^ for South
- Venu Mani^^^
- Raw Burmese Ruby
- Boar Pearl^^^

- Protection Bug Fossil^^^
- Jungli Kaali Billi ki Jer*^^
- Kamakhaya Sindhoor
- Gaj Mukta^^^
- Jungli Suar ka Daant
- Gemstones & Crystals:-
  - ➤ Qabana Stone^^
  - ➤ Wolk Stone^^
  - ➤ Heart Shaped Coral
- Rudrakshas:-
  - ➤ 19 Mukhi Rudraksha^^
  - ➤ 26 Mukhi Rudraksha^^
  - ➤ 28 Mukhi Rudraksha^^

Remedies of Cash Box, Locker, Safe in South-West

- Secret Programmed Vastu Diviner^^ for South-West
- Rahu ki Kaudi
- Venu Mani^^^
- Naagmani Glowing^^
- Jungli Kaali Billi ki Jer*^^
- Hatha Jodi Jadh Samet (With Root)
- Protection Bug Fossil^^^
- Boar Pearl^^^
- Talismani Mani for Enemies
- Antrikha / Space Stone / Space Stone Antrikha^^^
- Sher ka Daant
- Shark Teeth
- Gaj Mukta^^^
- Gemstones & Crystals:-
  - ➤ Qabana Stone^^
  - ➤ Wolk Stone^^

- ➤ Grey Japanese Coral
- Rudrakshas:-
  - ➤ 19 Mukhi Rudraksha
  - ➤ 28 Mukhi Rudraksha^^
  - ➤ 29 Mukhi Rudraksha^^
  - ➤ 1 Mukhi Trinetra Rudraksha^^
  - ➤ 1 Mukhi Jyotir Lingum Rudraksha^^
  - ➤ Charam Pashupati Nath Rudraksha^^^

Remedies of Cash Box, Locker, Safe in North-West

- Secret Programmed Vastu Diviner^^ for North-West
- Megha Mani^^
- Moon Rock^
- Aakash Mani Nubh Mani^^
- Infinity Gem^^ (Faco Crystal) White
- Pearl Blisters
- Protection Bug Fossil^^^
- Bidaal Mani^^^
- Siyar Singhi Joda Male Female Pair
- White Gemstones & Crystals:-
  - ➤ Adra Stone^^
  - ➤ Fully Round Natural Pearl^
  - ➤ Mother of Pearl
  - ➤ Triphane Gemstone^^
- Rudraksha:-
  - ➤ 22 Mukhi Rudraksha^
  - ➤ 1 Mukhi Trinetra Rudraksha^^
  - ➤ 1 Mukhi Jyotir Lingum Rudraksha^^

Remedies for Big Tijori / Strong Room

In this section, we have provided the right vastu correction tools and vastu dosh nivaran products to be used to rectify ill effects of big tijori, strong rooms in wrong directions.

Remedies for Tijori or Safe Room in North, North-East, East, South East, West & North West

- Secret Programmed Vastu Diviner^^ for South-West & South
- Specially Formulated Vastu Dosh Nivaran Yantra^^ for South-West & South
- Kale Ghodhe ki Naal
- 3 Pieces of Antrikha / Space Stone / Space Stone Antrikha^^^
- Infinity Gem^^ (Faco Crystal) Green & White
- Vishnu Chakra Moti^^
- Combination of 20-140 Vastu Items & Products
- Fully Round Natural Pearl^
- Tutmak Stone^^^
- Timi Stone^^^
- Adra Stone^^^
- Enemy Stone^^^
- **Conk Stone^^^**
- Qabana Stone^^^
- Protection Bug Fossil^^^
- Eagle Stone^^^
- Triphane Gemstone^^ White & Yellow
- Cordierite^^
- 1 Mukhi Trinetra Rudraksha^^
- 1 Mukhi Jyotir Lingum Rudraksha^^
- 1 Mukhi Java Rudraksha^^
- 1 Mukhi Java Rudraksha Gehuaan Dana^^
- 3 pieces of Dhan ka Bandha*^

- Moon Rock^^
- Natural Pearl Blisters
- Rahu ki Kaudi
- Naagmani Glowing^^
- Jungli Kaali Billi ki Jer
- Jungli Suar ka Daant
- Deep Sea Corals
- Deep Sea Shells
- 21 pieces of Money Eggs^^
- 26 Mukhi Rudraksha
- Charam Pashupati Nath Rudraksha^^^

Remedies for Neeven, Foundation or the Base of the Plot

In this section, we have provided the right vastu correction tools and vastu dosh nivaran products to be used to rectify ill effects of vastu doshas present in the neeven, base and foundation of the plot or a dwelling.

- Combination of 120 Vastu Items & Products
- 9 or 12 Yellow Pyramids
- Secret Programmed Vastu Diviner *^^ for North-East
- Secret Programmed Vastu Diviner^^ for South-West
- Secret Programmed Vastu Diviner^^ for Brahmasthaan
- Indrajaal
- Protection Bug Fossil^^^
- Morogul Mani^
- Conk Pearl Gilabi Mani^^^
- Antrikha / Space Stone / Space Stone Antrikha*^^^
- Nav-Grah Pyramid Yantra
- Naagmani Glowing^^
- Kamakhya Sindhoor
- Sahastra Sampudh Mani^
- Parad Shivling
- Samudrik Mani^^
- Shwetark Ganpati
- Haldi ke Ganesh
- Kastoori
- Rahu ki Kaudi
- Venu Mani^^^
- Naagmani Black^^
- Jungli Kaali Billi ki Jer*^^

- Hatha Jodi Jadh Samet (With Root)
- Brahmajaal
- Boar Pearl^^^
- Parad Shivling
- Shwetark Ganpati
- Talismani Mani for Enemies
- Sher ka Daant
- Shark Teeth
- Gaj Mukta^^^
- Gems & Crystals:-
  - Conk Stone^^^
  - Yellow Triphane Gemstone^^
  - Oyester Pearl^^
  - Moti Mani^^
  - Samudrik Stone^^
  - Golden Yellow Japanese Coral
  - Qabana Stone^^
  - Wolk Stone^^
  - Grey Japanese Coral
- Rudraksha:-
  - 1 Mukhi Rudraksha Gole Dana
  - 21 Mukhi Rudraksha
  - Combination of 16 Mukhi Rudraksha + 17 Mukhi Rudraksha + 18 Mukhi Rudraksha
  - Charam Pashupati Nath Rudraksha
  - 1 Mukhi Java Rudraksha^^
  - 1 Mukhi Java Rudraksha Gehuaan Dana^^
  - 27 Mukhi Rudraksha
  - 19 Mukhi Rudraksha
  - 28 Mukhi Rudraksha^^
  - 29 Mukhi Rudraksha^^
  - 1 Mukhi Trinetra Rudraksha^^
  - 1 Mukhi Jyotir Lingum Rudraksha^^
- Kale Ghodhe ki Naal
- Nav-Grah Pyramid Yantra
- Infinity Gem^^ (Faco Crystal) White & Green

- Vishnu Chakra Moti^^
- Tutmak Stone^^
- Timi Stone^^^
- Adra Stone^^
- **Conk Stone^^^**
- Qabana Stone^^^
- Eagle Stone^^^
- Money Eggs^^
- Asphetic Shri Yantra
- Dhan ka Bandha*^

Remedies for Overhead Beams

In this section, we have provided the right vastu correction tools and vastu dosh nivaran products to be used to rectify ill effects of overhead beams in wrong directions.

Remedies for Overhead Beams in North-East
- 9 or 12 Yellow Pyramids
- Yellow Water Pyramid
- Pure Stone Pyramid
- Directional Healing Crystal for North-East
- Secret Programmed Vastu Diviner *^^ for North-East
- Specially Formulated Vastu Dosh Nivaran Yantra for North East *^
- Protection Bug Fossil^^^
- Morogul Mani^
- Yellow Color
- Antrikha / Space Stone / Space Stone Antrikha*^^^

- Samudrik Mani^^
- Shwetark Ganpati
- Haldi ke Ganesh
- Kastoori

Remedies for Overhead Beams in East
- Directional Healing Crystal for East
- Secret Programmed Vastu Diviner^^ for East
- Specially Formulated Vastu Dosh Nivaran Yantra*^ for East
- Morogul Mani^
- Pure Stone Pyramid
- 5 Orange Pyramids
- Orange Water Pyramid
- Sahastra Sampudh Mani^

Remedies for Overhead Beams in South-East
- Directional Healing Crystal for South-East
- Secret Programmed Vastu Diviner*^^ for South-East
- Specially Formulated Vastu Dosh Nivaran Yantra*^ for South-East
- Deep Sea Corals *(Specific Patterns Needed)**
- Deep Sea Shells *(Specific Patterns Needed)**
- Pure & Natural Crystal Balls
- White Flowers
- Boar Pearl^^^
- Protection Bug Fossil^^^
- Kaama Siyar Singhi
- Jungli Kaali Billi ki Jer*^^
- Kamakhaya Sindhoor

Remedies for Overhead Beams in South

- Directional Healing Crystal for South
- Secret Programmed Vastu Diviner^^ for South
- Specially Formulated Vastu Dosh Nivaran Yantra*^ for South
- Pure Stone Pyramid
- 8 Red Pyramids *
- Venu Mani^^^
- Raw Burmese Ruby
- Boar Pearl^^^
- Protection Bug Fossil^^^
- Jungli Kaali Billi ki Jer*^^
- Kamakhaya Sindhoor
- Gaj Mukta^^^
- Dakshinavarti Shankh

Remedies for Overhead Beams in South-West

- Directional Healing Crystal for South-West
- Secret Programmed Vastu Diviner^^ for South-West
- Specially Formulated Vastu Dosh Nivaran Yantra*^ for South-West
- Rahu ki Kaudi
- Venu Mani^^^
- Naagmani Glowing^^
- Jungli Kaali Billi ki Jer*^^
- Brahmajaal
- Protection Bug Fossil^^^
- Boar Pearl^^^
- Parad Shivling
- Talismani Mani for Enemies
- Antrikha / Space Stone / Space Stone Antrikha^^^
- Shark Teeth
- Gaj Mukta^^^

Remedies for Overhead Beams in West

- Blue Water Pyramid
- Directional Healing Crystal for West
- Secret Programmed Vastu Diviner^^ for West
- Specially Formulated Vastu Dosh Nivaran Yantra*^ for West
- Pure Stone Pyramid
- 10 or 11 Black / Blue Pyramids
- Morogul Mani^
- Conk Pearl Gilabi Mani^^^
- Raw Sugilite Crystal
- Raw Turquoise Crystals
- Narmadeshwar Shivling Black
- Saam Siyar Singhi
- Jungli Kaali Billi ki Jer*^^
- Gaj Mukta^^^
- Sahastra Sampudh Mani^
- Dhan ka Bandha^
- Samudrik Mani^^

Remedies for Overhead Beams in North-West

- Directional Healing Crystal for North-West
- Secret Programmed Vastu Diviner^^ for North-West
- Megha Mani^^
- Moon Rock^
- Aakash Mani Nubh Mani^^
- Pearl Blisters
- Protection Bug Fossil^^^
- Bidaal Mani^^^
- Siyar Singhi Joda Male Female Pair

Remedies for Overhead Beams in North

- Green Water Pyramid
- Directional Healing Crystal for North
- Secret Programmed Vastu Diviner^^ for North
- Specially Formulated Vastu Dosh Nivaran Yantra*^ for North
- Money Eggs^^
- Morogul Mani^
- Samudrik Mani^^
- Raw Emerald
- Conk Pearl Gilabi Mani^^^
- Jungli Kaali Billi ki Jer*^^
- Saam Siyar Singhi
- Sahastra Sampudh Mani^
- Dhan ka Bandha*^
- Asphetic Shri Yantra

Remedies for Overhead Beams in Bhrahmasthan

- Secret Programmed Vastu Diviner^^ for Brahmasthaan
- Specially Formulated Vastu Dosh Nivaran Yantra^^ for Brahmasthaan
- Kale Ghodhe ki Naal
- Nav-Grah Pyramid Yantra
- Antrikha / Space Stone / Space Stone Antrikha^^^
- Vishnu Chakra Moti^^
- Combination of 120 Vastu Items & Products
- Fully Round Natural Pearl^^
- Tutmak Stone^^
- Timi Stone^^^
- Adra Stone^^
- Enemy Stone^^

- **Conk Stone^^^**
- Qabana Stone^^^
- Protection Bug Fossil^^^
- Eagle Stone^^^
- Triphane Gemstone ^^
- Cordierite^^
- Nagmani Black^
- Naagmani Glowing^^^
- Deep Sea Corals^
- Deep Sea Shells^
- Money Eggs^^
- Kastoori
- Dhan ka Bandha*^
- Moon Rock^^
- Natural Pearl Blisters

Remedies for House & Commercial Establishments Surrounded by Big Buildings

In this section, we have provided the right vastu correction tools and vastu dosh nivaran products to be used to rectify ill effects of a house and commercial establishment surrounded by big buildings.

Remedies for House surrounded by Big Buildings in North-East

- Secret Programmed Vastu Diviner *^^ for North-East
- Specially Formulated Vastu Dosh Nivaran Yantra for North East *^
- Protection Bug Fossil^^^
- Morogul Mani^
- Conk Pearl Gilabi Mani^^^
- Antrikha / Space Stone / Space Stone Antrikha*^^^
- Naagmani Glowing^^

- Sahastra Sampudh Mani^
- Samudrik Mani^^
- Kastoori
- Rudrakshas:-
  - ➢ 9 Mukhi Rudraksha
  - ➢ 12 Mukhi Rudraksha
  - ➢ 18 Mukhi Rudraksha
  - ➢ 27 Mukhi Rudraksha

Remedies for House surrounded by Big Buildings in North

- Secret Programmed Vastu Diviner^^ for North
- Specially Formulated Vastu Dosh Nivaran Yantra*^ for North
- Money Eggs^^
- Morogul Mani^
- Samudrik Mani^^
- Conk Pearl Gilabi Mani^^^
- Jungli Kaali Billi ki Jer*^^
- Hatha Jodi with Actual Root
- Saam Siyar Singhi
- Sahastra Sampudh Mani^
- Dhan ka Bandha*^
- Rudraksha:-
  - ➢ 3 Mukhi Rudraksha
  - ➢ 6 Mukhi Rudraksha
  - ➢ 15 Mukhi Rudraksha
  - ➢ 21 Mukhi Rudraksha^
  - ➢ 25 Mukhi Rudraksha^^
  - ➢ 30 Mukhi Rudraksha^^

Remedies for House surrounded by Big Buildings in East

- Secret Programmed Vastu Diviner^^ for East
- Specially Formulated Vastu Dosh Nivaran Yantra*^ for East
- Education Tower
- Morogul Mani^
- Sahastra Sampudh Mani^
- Conk Pearl Gilabi Mani^^^
- Sher Ka Daant (Lions Teeth)
- Junglee Suar ka Daant (Wild Pig Teeth)
- Rudrakshas:-
  - 5 Mukhi Rudraksha
  - 14 Mukhi Rudraksha
  - 23 Mukhi Rudraksha

Remedies for Large Factories, Manufacturing Units & Industrial Units

In this section, we have provided the right vastu correction tools and vastu dosh nivaran products to be used to rectify ill effects particular directions in large factories, manufacturing and industrial units.

Remedies for Healing East Direction

- Directional Healing Crystal for East
- Secret Programmed Vastu Diviner^^ for East
- Specially Formulated Vastu Dosh Nivaran Yantra*^ for East
- Education Tower
- Morogul Mani^
- Pure Stone Pyramid
- 5 Orange Pyramids
- Orange Water Pyramid
- Sahastra Sampudh Mani^

- Water Charging Crystals
- Negativity Cleaning Crystals
- Salt Lamp
- Conk Pearl Gilabi Mani^^^
- Orange Color
- Infinity Gem^^ (Faco Crystal) Green
- Sher Ka Daant (Lions Teeth)
- Junglee Suar ka Daant (Wild Pig Teeth)
- Gems & Crystals:-
  - Orange Sunstone
  - Orange Topaz
  - Orange Tourmaline
  - Orange Garnet
  - Orange Opal
  - Conk Stone^^^
  - Orange Sphalerite
  - Orange Flourite
  - Carnelian
  - Oyester Pearl^^
  - Moti Mani^^
  - Orange Agate
  - Peach Aventurine
  - Orange Beryl
  - Orange Citrine
  - Samudrik Stone^^
  - Amber
- Rudrakshas:-
  - 5 Mukhi Rudraksha
  - 14 Mukhi Rudraksha
  - 23 Mukhi Rudraksha
- Sampoorna Vastu Dosh Nivaran Kit of 120+ Vastu Healing Items & Products

Remedies for Healing South Direction
- Directional Healing Crystal for South

- Secret Programmed Vastu Diviner^^ for South
- Specially Formulated Vastu Dosh Nivaran Yantra*^ for South
- Negativity Cleaning Crystals
- Salt Lamp
- Pure Stone Pyramid
- 8 Red Pyramids *
- Red Color
- Venu Mani^^^
- Raw Burmese Ruby
- Boar Pearl^^^
- Protection Bug Fossil^^^
- Red Lord Hanuman Photo / Idol
- Hatha Jodi Actual with Root
- Jungli Kaali Billi ki Jer*^^
- Kamakhaya Sindhoor
- Shwetark Ganpati
- Gaj Mukta^^^
- Jungli Suar ka Daant
- Dakshinavarti Shankh
- Sampoorna Vastu Dosh Nivaran Kit of 120+ Vastu Healing Items & Products
- Red Gemstones & Crystals:-
  - ➢ Carnelian
  - ➢ Red Garnet
  - ➢ Qabana Stone^^
  - ➢ Red Jasper
  - ➢ Red Agate
  - ➢ Red Fluorite
  - ➢ Wolk Stone^^
  - ➢ Red Sapphire
  - ➢ Red Spinel
  - ➢ Red Coral
  - ➢ Heart Shaped Coral
- Rudrakshas:-
  - ➢ 1 Mukhi Rudraksha

- ➤ 8 Mukhi Rudraksha
- ➤ 17 Mukhi Rudraksha
- ➤ 19 Mukhi Rudraksha^^
- ➤ 26 Mukhi Rudraksha^^
- ➤ 28 Mukhi Rudraksha^^

Remedies for Healing West Direction

- Blue Water Pyramid
- Directional Healing Crystal for West
- Secret Programmed Vastu Diviner^^ for West
- Specially Formulated Vastu Dosh Nivaran Yantra*^ for West
- Pure Stone Pyramid
- 10 or 11 Black / Blue Pyramids
- Water Charging Crystals
- Negativity Cleaning Crystals
- Salt Lamp
- Morogul Mani^
- Conk Pearl Gilabi Mani^^^
- Education Tower
- Raw Sugilite Crystal
- Raw Turquoise Crystals
- Black & Blue Colors
- Infinity Gem^^ (Faco Crystal) Green
- Narmadeshwar Shivling Black
- Saam Siyar Singhi
- Jungli Kaali Billi ki Jer*^^
- Hatha Jodi
- Gaj Mukta^^^
- Dakshinavarti Shankh
- Sahastra Sampudh Mani^
- Dhan ka Bandha^
- Samudrik Mani^^
- Gemstones & Crystals:-

- ➢ Lapis Lazuli
- ➢ Hematite
- ➢ Angelite
- ➢ Oyester Pearl^^
- ➢ Moti Mani^^
- ➢ Black Obsidian
- ➢ Blue Tourmaline
- ➢ Aquamarine
- ➢ Blue Agate
- ➢ Black Agate
- ➢ Iolite
- ➢ Conk Stone^^^
- ➢ Sodalite
- ➢ Blue Fluorite
- ➢ Blue Amber
- ➢ Azurite
- ➢ Black Opal
- ➢ Black Pearl
- ➢ Black Onyx
- ➢ Black Tourmaline
- ➢ Kyanite
- ➢ Cordierite
- ➢ Samudrik Stone^^
- ➢ Purple Sapphire
- ➢ Japanese Blue Coral
- ➢ Japanese Black Coral
- ➢ Black Spinel
- Rudraksha:-
  - ➢ 10 Mukhi Rudraksha
  - ➢ 11 Mukhi Rudraksha
  - ➢ 19 Mukhi Rudraksha
  - ➢ 28 Mukhi Rudraksha^^
  - ➢ 29 Mukhi Rudraksha^^
  - ➢ 1 Mukhi Trinetra Rudraksha^^
  - ➢ 1 Mukhi Jyotir Lingum Rudraksha^^
- Sampoorna Vastu Dosh Nivaran Kit of 120+ Vastu Healing Items & Products

Remedies for Healing North Direction

- Green Water Pyramid
- Directional Healing Crystal for North
- Secret Programmed Vastu Diviner^^ for North
- Specially Formulated Vastu Dosh Nivaran Yantra*^ for North
- Water Charging Crystals
- Negativity Cleaning Crystals
- Salt Lamp
- Pure Stone Pyramid
- 3 or 6 Green Pyramids
- Money Eggs^^
- Infinity Gem^^ (Faco Crystal) Green
- Morogul Mani^
- Green Color
- Plants
- Samudrik Mani^^
- Raw Emerald
- Conk Pearl Gilabi Mani^^^
- Indrajaal, Brahmajaal
- Jungli Kaali Billi ki Jer*^^
- Hatha Jodi with Actual Root
- Saam Siyar Singhi
- Sahastra Sampudh Mani^
- Dakshinavarti Shankh
- Dhan ka Bandha*^
- Asphetic Shri Yantra
- Sampoorna Vastu Dosh Nivaran Kit of 120+ Vastu Healing Items & Products
- Gemstones & Crystals:-
  - ➢ Green Jade
  - ➢ Conk Stone^^^
  - ➢ Green Aventurine

204

- ➢ Green Agate
- ➢ Green Garnet
- ➢ Green Tourmaline
- ➢ Peridot
- ➢ Hiddenite^
- ➢ Green Amber
- ➢ Green Turquoise
- ➢ Malachite
- ➢ Oyester Pearl^^
- ➢ Moti Mani^^
- ➢ Green Fluorite
- ➢ Green Jasper
- ➢ Amazonite
- ➢ Florite
- ➢ Samudrik Stone^^
- ➢ Parasha Gemstone^^^
- ➢ Green Tourmaline
- ➢ Green Beryl^
- Rudraksha:-
  - ➢ 3 Mukhi Rudraksha
  - ➢ 6 Mukhi Rudraksha
  - ➢ 15 Mukhi Rudraksha
  - ➢ 21 Mukhi Rudraksha^
  - ➢ 25 Mukhi Rudraksha^^
  - ➢ 30 Mukhi Rudraksha^^

Remedies for Healing Bhrahmasthan

- Secret Programmed Vastu Diviner^^ for Brahmasthaan
- Specially Formulated Vastu Dosh Nivaran Yantra^^ for Brahmasthaan
- Kale Ghodhe ki Naal
- Nav-Grah Pyramid Yantra
- Antrikha / Space Stone / Space Stone Antrikha^^^
- Infinity Gem^^ (Faco Crystal) White & Green
- Vishnu Chakra Moti^^

- Combination of 120 Vastu Items & Products
- Fully Round Natural Pearl^^
- Tutmak Stone^^
- Timi Stone^^^
- Adra Stone^^
- Enemy Stone^^
- **Conk Stone^^^**
- Qabana Stone^^^
- Protection Bug Fossil^^^
- Eagle Stone^^^
- Triphane Gemstone ^^
- Cordierite^^
- Nagmani Black^
- Naagmani Glowing^^^
- Combination of Brahmajaal + Indrajaal
- Combination of Kaali Billi ki Jer + Siyar Singhi + Mota Hatha Jodi
- Kamakhaya Sindoor
- Parad Shivling
- Deep Sea Corals^
- Deep Sea Shells^
- Money Eggs^^
- Combination of 120-140 Vastu Healing Products
- Kastoori
- Asphetic Shri Yantra
- Dhan ka Bandha*^
- Moon Rock^^
- Natural Pearl Blisters
- Rudraksha:-
  - 1 Mukhi Rudraksha Gole Dana
  - 21 Mukhi Rudraksha
  - Combination of 16 Mukhi Rudraksha + 17 Mukhi Rudraksha + 18 Mukhi Rudraksha
  - Charam Pashupati Nath Rudraksha
    1 Mukhi Java Rudraksha^^

➤ 1 Mukhi Java Rudraksha Gehuaan Dana^^
- Gemstones: Hiddenite, Parasha, Green Beryl, Green Florite, Yellow Florspar, Yellow Beryl, Yellow Spodumene, Scapolite, White Beryl

Remedies for Large Open Compounds

In this section, we have provided the right vastu correction tools and vastu dosh nivaran products to be used to rectify ill effects of large open compounds in wrong directions.

Remedies for Large Open Compounds in South
Rudrakshas:-
- ➤ 1 Mukhi Rudraksha
- ➤ 8 Mukhi Rudraksha
- ➤ 17 Mukhi Rudraksha
- ➤ 19 Mukhi Rudraksha^^
- ➤ 26 Mukhi Rudraksha^^
- ➤ 28 Mukhi Rudraksha^^

Remedies for Large Open Compounds in South-West
Rudrakshas:-
- ➤ 10 Mukhi Rudraksha

- ➤ 11 Mukhi Rudraksha
- ➤ 19 Mukhi Rudraksha
- ➤ 28 Mukhi Rudraksha^^
- ➤ 29 Mukhi Rudraksha^^
- ➤ 1 Mukhi Trinetra Rudraksha^^
- ➤ 1 Mukhi Jyotir Lingum Rudraksha^^
- ➤ Charam Pashupati Nath Rudraksha^^^

Remedies for Large Open Compounds in West
Rudraksha:-
- ➤ 10 Mukhi Rudraksha
- ➤ 11 Mukhi Rudraksha
- ➤ 19 Mukhi Rudraksha
- ➤ 28 Mukhi Rudraksha^^
- ➤ 29 Mukhi Rudraksha^^
- ➤ 1 Mukhi Trinetra Rudraksha^^
- ➤ 1 Mukhi Jyotir Lingum Rudraksha^^

Remedies for Large Housing Societies

In this section, we have provided the right vastu correction tools and vastu dosh nivaran products to be used to rectify ill effects of large housing societies in wrong directions.

Remedies for Healing North-East Direction
- 120 Yellow Pyramids
- 12 Pure Stone Pyramids
- 12 Secret Programmed Vastu Diviner *^^ for North-East
- Specially Formulated Vastu Dosh Nivaran Yantra for North East *^
- 12 Brahmajaal
- 12 Protection Bug Fossils^^^
- 12 Morogul Mani^
- 12 Conk Pearl Gilabi Mani^^^
- 12 Antrikha / Space Stone / Space Stone Antrikha*^^^
- 12 Nav-Grah Pyramid Yantra
- 12 Naagmani Glowing^^

- 12 Sahastra Sampudh Mani^
- 12 Parad Shivling
- 12 Samudrik Mani^^
- 12 Shwetark Ganpati Carved
- 12 Haldi ke Ganesh
- 12 Kastoori
- Sampoorna Vastu Dosh Nivaran Kit of 120+ Vastu Healing Items & Products

Remedies for Healing East Direction

- 5 Secret Programmed Vastu Diviner^^ for East
- 5 Specially Formulated Vastu Dosh Nivaran Yantra*^ for East
- 5 Education Tower
- 5 Morogul Mani^
- 5 Sahastra Sampudh Mani^
- 5 Conk Pearl Gilabi Mani^^^
- 5 Infinity Gem^^ (Faco Crystal) Green
- Sampoorna Vastu Dosh Nivaran Kit of 120+ Vastu Healing Items & Products

Remedies for Healing South-East Direction

- 7 Secret Programmed Vastu Diviner*^^ for South-East
- 7 Specially Formulated Vastu Dosh Nivaran Yantra*^ for South-East
- 7 Deep Sea Corals *(Specific Patterns Needed)**
- 7 Deep Sea Shells *(Specific Patterns Needed)**
- 7 Boar Pearl^^^
- 7 Protection Bug Fossil^^^
- 7 Bidaal Mani^^^
- 7 Sterling Silver Artifacts
- 7 Infinity Gem^^ (Faco Crystal) White

- 7 Kaama Siyar Singhi
- 7 Jungli Kaali Billi ki Jer*^^
- Sampoorna Vastu Dosh Nivaran Kit of 120+ Vastu Healing Items & Products

Remedies for Healing South Direction

- 8 Secret Programmed Vastu Diviner^^ for South
- 8 Specially Formulated Vastu Dosh Nivaran Yantra*^ for South
- 8 Venu Mani^^^
- 8 Raw Burmese Ruby
- 8 Boar Pearl^^^
- 8 Protection Bug Fossil^^^
- 8 Jungli Kaali Billi ki Jer*^^
- 8 Shwetark Ganpati
- 8 Gaj Mukta^^^
- 8 Dakshinavarti Shankh
- Sampoorna Vastu Dosh Nivaran Kit of 120+ Vastu Healing Items & Products

Remedies for Healing South-West Direction

- 11 Secret Programmed Vastu Diviner^^ for South-West
- 11 Specially Formulated Vastu Dosh Nivaran Yantra*^ for South-West
- 11 Rahu ki Kaudi
- 11 Venu Mani^^^
- 11 Naagmani Glowing^^
- 11 Jungli Kaali Billi ki Jer*^^
- 11 Hatha Jodi Jadh Samet (With Root)
- 11 Brahmajaal
- 11 Protection Bug Fossil^^^
- 11 Boar Pearl^^^

- 11 Parad Shivling
- 11 Shwetark Ganpati
- 11 Talismani Mani for Enemies
- 11 Antrikha / Space Stone / Space Stone Antrikha^^^
- 11 Gaj Mukta^^^
- Sampoorna Vastu Dosh Nivaran Kit of 120+ Vastu Healing Items & Products

Remedies for Healing West Direction

- 10 Secret Programmed Vastu Diviner^^ for West
- 10 Specially Formulated Vastu Dosh Nivaran Yantra*^ for West
- 10 Morogul Mani^
- 10 Conk Pearl Gilabi Mani^^^
- 10 Education Tower
- 10 Raw Sugilite Crystal
- 10 Raw Turquoise Crystals
- 10 Infinity Gem^^ (Faco Crystal) Green
- 10 Narmadeshwar Shivling Black
- 10 Saam Siyar Singhi
- 10 Jungli Kaali Billi ki Jer*^^
- 10 Gaj Mukta^^^
- 10 Sahastra Sampudh Mani^
- 10 Dhan ka Bandha^
- 10 Samudrik Mani^^
- Sampoorna Vastu Dosh Nivaran Kit of 120+ Vastu Healing Items & Products

Remedies for Healing North-West Direction

- 4 Secret Programmed Vastu Diviner^^ for North-West
- 4 Negativity Cleaning Crystals

- 4 Megha Mani^^
- 4 Pure Stone Pyramid
- 4 Moon Rock^
- 4 Aakash Mani Nubh Mani^^
- 4 Infinity Gem^^ (Faco Crystal) White
- 4 Narmadeshwar Shivling White
- 4 Pearl Blisters
- 4 Protection Bug Fossil^^^
- 4 Bidaal Mani^^^
- 4 Siyar Singhi Joda Male Female Pair
- Sampoorna Vastu Dosh Nivaran Kit of 120+ Vastu Healing Items & Products

Remedies for Healing North Direction

- 6 Secret Programmed Vastu Diviner^^ for North
- 6 Specially Formulated Vastu Dosh Nivaran Yantra*^ for North
- 6 Money Eggs^^
- 6 Infinity Gem^^ (Faco Crystal) Green
- 6 Morogul Mani^
- 6 Samudrik Mani^^
- 6 Raw Emerald
- 6 Conk Pearl Gilabi Mani^^^
- 6 Jungli Kaali Billi ki Jer*^^
- 6 Saam Siyar Singhi
- 6 Sahastra Sampudh Mani^
- 6 Dhan ka Bandha*^
- 6 Asphetic Shri Yantra
- Sampoorna Vastu Dosh Nivaran Kit of 120+ Vastu Healing Items & Products

Remedies for Healing Bhrahmasthan

- 9 Secret Programmed Vastu Diviner^^ for Brahmasthaan
- 9 Specially Formulated Vastu Dosh Nivaran Yantra^^ for Brahmasthaan
- 9 Kale Ghodhe ki Naal
- 9 Nav-Grah Pyramid Yantra
- 9 Antrikha / Space Stone / Space Stone Antrikha^^^
- 9 Infinity Gem^^ (Faco Crystal) White & Green
- 9 Vishnu Chakra Moti^^
- 9 Combination of 120 Vastu Items & Products
- 9 Fully Round Natural Pearl^^
- 9 Tutmak Stone^^
- 9 Timi Stone^^^
- 9 Adra Stone^^
- 9 Enemy Stone^^
- 9 **Conk Stone^^^**
- 9 Qabana Stone^^^
- 9 Protection Bug Fossil^^^
- 9 Eagle Stone^^^
- 9 Triphane Gemstone ^^
- 9 Cordierite^^
- 9 Nagmani Black^
- 9 Naagmani Glowing^^^
- Combination of Brahmajaal + Indrajaal
- 9 Combination of Kaali Billi ki Jer + Siyar Singhi + Mota Hatha Jodi
- 9 Parad Shivling
- 9 Deep Sea Corals^
- 9 Deep Sea Shells^
- 9 Money Eggs^^
- Combination of 120-140 Vastu Healing Products
- 9 Kastoori
- 9 Asphetic Shri Yantra

- 9 Dhan ka Bandha*^
- 9 Moon Rock^^
- 9 Natural Pearl Blisters

Remedies for Vacant & Unconstructed Plots

In this section, we have provided the right vastu correction tools and vastu dosh nivaran products to be used to rectify ill effects of all types of vastu doshas of vacant and unconstructed plots.

Remedies to be placed in a big pit in the centre of the Plot

*   Secret Programmed Vastu Diviner^^ for Brahmasthaan
*   Specially Formulated Vastu Dosh Nivaran Yantra^^ for Brahmasthaan
*   Kale Ghodhe ki Naal
*   Antrikha / Space Stone / Space Stone Antrikha^^^
*   Infinity Gem^^ (Faco Crystal) Green
*   Infinity Gem^^ (Faco Crystal) White
*   Vishnu Chakra Moti^^
*   Combination of 20-140 Vastu Items & Products
*   Fully Round Natural Pearl^
*   Tutmak Stone (Fish Pearl)
*   Timi Stone (Whale Pearl)
*   Adra Stone
*   Enemy Stone
*   Conk Stone
*   Qabana Stone
*   Protection Bug Fossil^^^
*   Eagle Stone^^^
*   Triphane Gemstone ^^
*   Cordierite^^
*   22 Mukhi to 28 Mukhi Rudraksha^^
*   1 Mukhi Trinetra Rudraksha^^
*   1 Mukhi Jyotir Lingum Rudraksha^^
*   1 Mukhi Java Rudraksha^^

- 1 Mukhi Java Rudraksha Gehuaan Dana^^
- Dhan ka Bandha*^
- Moon Rock^^
- Natural Pearl Blisters
- Parad Shivling, Shwetark Ganpati, Haldi ke Ganesh, Kastoori
- Kamakhya Sindhoor, Kamiya Sindhoor
- Pure Stone Pyramid
- Rahu ki Kaudi
- Naagmani Glowing^^
- Jungli Kaali Billi ki Jer
- Jungli Suar ka Daant
- Deep Sea Corals
- Deep Sea Shells
- Kaali Billi ki Jer*^^
- Japanese Blue Coral
- Japanese Black Coral
- Money Eggs^^
- Charam Pashupati Nath Rudraksha^^^

Remedies of Unwanted Open Space

In this section, we have provided the right vastu correction tools and vastu dosh nivaran products to be used to rectify ill effects of unwanted open spaces in wrong directions.

Remedies of Unwanted Open Space in South

- Secret Programmed Vastu Diviner^^ for South
- Specially Formulated Vastu Dosh Nivaran Yantra*^ for South
- Negativity Cleaning Crystals
- Salt Lamp
- Pure Stone Pyramid
- 8 Rcd Pyramids *
- Rcd Color
- Venu Mani^^^
- Raw Burmese Ruby

Remedies of Unwanted Open Space in South-West

- Secret Programmed Vastu Diviner^^ for South-West
- Specially Formulated Vastu Dosh Nivaran Yantra*^ for South-West
- Negativity Cleaning Crystals
- Salt Lamp
- Pure Stone Pyramid
- 10 or 11 Brown Pyramids
- Rahu ki Kaudi
- Venu Mani^^^
- Brown & Grey Colors

Remedies of Unwanted Open Space in West

- Blue Water Pyramid
- Directional Healing Crystal for West
- Secret Programmed Vastu Diviner^^ for West
- Specially Formulated Vastu Dosh Nivaran Yantra*^ for West
- Pure Stone Pyramid
- 10 or 11 Black / Blue Pyramids
- Water Charging Crystals
- Negativity Cleaning Crystals
- Salt Lamp
- Morogul Mani^

Remedies of Unwanted Open Space in North-West

- Secret Programmed Vastu Diviner^^ for North-West
- Negativity Cleaning Crystals
- Salt Lamp
- Megha Mani^^
- Pure Stone Pyramid
- 4 White Pyramids
- Moon Rock^
- Aakash Mani Nubh Mani^^

Remedies of Unwanted Open Space in South-East

- Secret Programmed Vastu Diviner*^^ for South-East
- Specially Formulated Vastu Dosh Nivaran Yantra*^ for South-East
- Deep Sea Corals *(Specific Patterns Needed)**
- Deep Sea Shells *(Specific Patterns Needed)**
- Pure & Natural Crystal Balls
- Boar Pearl^^^

- Protection Bug Fossil^^^

Remedies of Closed, Heavy & Dark Spaces

In this section, we have provided the right vastu correction tools and vastu dosh nivaran products to be used to rectify ill effects of closed, heavy and dark spaces in wrong directions.

Remedies of Unwanted Closed, Heavy & Dark Space in North-East

- Secret Programmed Vastu Diviner *^^ for North-East
- Specially Formulated Vastu Dosh Nivaran Yantra for North East *^
- Protection Bug Fossil^^^
- Morogul Mani^
- Antrikha / Space Stone / Space Stone Antrikha*^^^
- Samudrik Mani^^
- 18 Mukhi Rudraksha
- 27 Mukhi Rudraksha

Remedies of Unwanted Closed, Heavy & Dark Space in East

- Secret Programmed Vastu Diviner^^ for East
- Specially Formulated Vastu Dosh Nivaran Yantra*^ for East
- Morogul Mani^
- Sahastra Sampudh Mani^

- Infinity Gem^^ (Faco Crystal) Green
- 14 Mukhi Rudraksha
- 23 Mukhi Rudraksha

Remedies of Unwanted Closed, Heavy & Dark Space in North

- Secret Programmed Vastu Diviner^^ for North
- Specially Formulated Vastu Dosh Nivaran Yantra*^ for North
- Money Eggs^^
- Infinity Gem^^ (Faco Crystal) Green
- Morogul Mani^
- Plants
- Samudrik Mani^^
- Jungli Kaali Billi ki Jer*^^
- Saam Siyar Singhi
- Sahastra Sampudh Mani^
- Dhan ka Bandha*^
- 15 Mukhi Rudraksha
- 21 Mukhi Rudraksha^
- 25 Mukhi Rudraksha^^
- 30 Mukhi Rudraksha^^

Remedies of Unwanted Closed, Heavy & Dark Space in North-West

- Secret Programmed Vastu Diviner^^ for North-West
- Megha Mani^^
- Moon Rock^
- Aakash Mani Nubh Mani^^
- Infinity Gem^^ (Faco Crystal) White
- Pearl Blisters
- Protection Bug Fossil^^^

- Bidaal Mani^^^
- 13 Mukhi Rudraksha
- 22 Mukhi Rudraksha^
- 1 Mukhi Trinetra Rudraksha^^
- 1 Mukhi Jyotir Lingum Rudraksha^^

Remedies of Unwanted Closed, Heavy & Dark Space in South-East

- Secret Programmed Vastu Diviner*^^ for South-East
- Specially Formulated Vastu Dosh Nivaran Yantra*^ for South-East
- Deep Sea Corals *(Specific Patterns Needed)*
- Deep Sea Shells *(Specific Patterns Needed)*
- Boar Pearl^^^
- Protection Bug Fossil^^^
- Bidaal Mani^^^
- Infinity Gem^^ (Faco Crystal) White
- Kaama Siyar Singhi
- Jungli Kaali Billi ki Jer*^^
- 1 Mukhi Trinetra Rudraksha^^
- 1 Mukhi Jyotir Lingum Rudraksha^^
- 16 Mukhi Rudraksha
- 20 Mukhi Rudraksha
- 25 Mukhi Rudraksha^^

Part 2

Remedies for Getting Financial & Monetary Gains, Higher Income, Cash Inflow, Huge Savings & Good Investments

In this section, we have provided the right vastu correction tools and vastu dosh nivaran products to be used to get financial and monetary gains, higher income, cash inflow, huge savings and good investments.

- Secret Programmed Vastu Diviner^^ for North
- Specially Formulated Vastu Dosh Nivaran Yantra*^ for North
- Pure Stone Pyramid
- Money Eggs^^

- Infinity Gem^^ (Faco Crystal) Green
- Morogul Mani^
- Green Color
- Plants
- Samudrik Mani^^
- Raw Emerald
- Conk Pearl Gilabi Mani^^^
- Jungli Kaali Billi ki Jer*^^
- Saam Siyar Singhi
- Sahastra Sampudh Mani^
- Dakshinavarti Shankh
- Dhan ka Bandha*^
- Combination of 120-140 Vastu Healing Products to be placed in North Direction.
- Gemstones & Crystals:-
  - Conk Stone^^^
  - Hiddenite^
  - Oyester Pearl^^
  - Moti Mani^^
  - Samudrik Stone^^
  - Parasha Gemstone^^^
  - Green Beryl^
- Rudraksha:-
  - 15 Mukhi Rudraksha
  - 21 Mukhi Rudraksha^
  - 25 Mukhi Rudraksha^^
  - 30 Mukhi Rudraksha^^

Remedies for Health Issues, Depression & Chronic Diseases, Problems to Male Members of the House, Multiple Deaths of Male Members of the House, Unnecessary Fear, Headaches, Unexpected & Extreme Losses, More of New Born Female Babies Instead of Boy Child, For Overall Prosperity, Higher Satisfaction, Peace & Harmony in Life

In this section, we have provided the right vastu correction tools and vastu dosh nivaran products to be used as remedies for health issues, depression & chronic diseases, problems to male members of the house, multiple deaths of male members of the house, unnecessary fear, headaches, unexpected & extreme losses, more of new born female babies instead of boy child, for overall prosperity, higher satisfaction, peace

& harmony in life

- Secret Programmed Vastu Diviner^^ for Brahmasthaan
- Specially Formulated Vastu Dosh Nivaran Yantra^^ for Brahmasthaan
- Secret Programmed Vastu Diviner *^^ for North-East
- Specially Formulated Vastu Dosh Nivaran Yantra for North East *^
- Infinity Gem^^ (Faco Crystal) White & Green
- Vishnu Chakra Moti^^
- Fully Round Natural Pearl^^
- Tutmak Stone^^
- Timi Stone^^^
- Adra Stone^^
- Enemy Stone^^
- **Conk Stone^^^**
- Qabana Stone^^^
- Protection Bug Fossil^^^
- Eagle Stone^^^
- Triphane Gemstone ^^
- Cordierite^^
- Nagmani Black^
- Naagmani Glowing^^^
- Deep Sea Corals^
- Deep Sea Shells^
- Money Eggs^^
- Natural Pearl Blisters
- Protection Bug Fossil^^^
- Morogul Mani^
- Conk Pearl Gilabi Mani^^^
- Antrikha / Space Stone / Space Stone Antrikha*^^^
- Sahastra Sampudh Mani^

- Parad Shivling
- Samudrik Mani^^
- Gems & Crystals:-
  - Conk Stone^^^
  - Yellow Triphane Gemstone^^
  - Oyester Pearl^^
  - Moti Mani^^
  - Yellow Florspar
  - Yellow Spodumene
  - Yellow Beryl
  - Scapolite
  - Samudrik Stone^^
  - Golden Yellow Japanese Coral
- 1 Mukhi Rudraksha Gole Dana
- 21 Mukhi Rudraksha
- Combination of 16 Mukhi Rudraksha + 17 Mukhi Rudraksha + 18 Mukhi Rudraksha
- Charam Pashupati Nath Rudraksha
- 1 Mukhi Java Rudraksha Gehuaan Dana^^
- 27 Mukhi Rudraksha
- Combination of 120-140 Vastu Healing Products to be placed in North-East Direction.

Remedies for Childbirth, Childlessness & Progeny

In this section, we have provided the right vastu correction tools and vastu dosh nivaran products to be used as remedies for childbirth, childlessness and progeny.

- Megha Mani^^
- Moon Rock^
- Aakash Mani Nubh Mani^^
- Infinity Gem^^ (Faco Crystal) White
- Pearl Blisters
- Protection Bug Fossil^^^
- Bidaal Mani^^^
- Siyar Singhi Joda Male Female Pair
- Morogul Mani^
- Conk Pearl Gilabi Mani^^^
- Antrikha / Space Stone / Space Stone Antrikha*^^^
- Naagmani Glowing^^

- Sahastra Sampudh Mani^
- Samudrik Mani^^
- Combination of 120-140 Vastu Healing Products to be placed in North-East Direction.
- Gems & Crystals:-
  - Conk Stone^^^
  - Oyester Pearl^^
  - Adra Stone^^
  - Fully Round Natural Pearl^
  - Triphane Gemstone^^
  - Moti Mani^^
  - Yellow Florspar
  - Yellow Spodumene
  - Yellow Beryl
  - Scapolite
  - Samudrik Stone^^
  - Golden Yellow Japanese Coral
- Rudraksha:-
  - 13 Mukhi Rudraksha
  - 18 Mukhi Rudraksha
  - 22 Mukhi Rudraksha^
  - 27 Mukhi Rudraksha
  - 1 Mukhi Trinetra Rudraksha^^
  - 1 Mukhi Jyotir Lingum Rudraksha^^

Remedies for Birth of a Male Child (Son)

In this section, we have provided the right vastu correction tools and vastu dosh nivaran products to be used as remedies for birth of a male child, a son.

- Paasha Jaal
- Paaras Booti
- Garuda Mani
- Megha Mani^^
- Moon Rock^
- Aakash Mani Nubh Mani^^
- Infinity Gem^^ (Faco Crystal) White & Green
- Pearl Blisters
- Protection Bug Fossil^^^
- Bidaal Mani^^^
- Siyar Singhi Joda Male Female Pair
- Morogul Mani^
- Conk Pearl Gilabi Mani^^^
- Antrikha / Space Stone / Space Stone Antrikha*^^^
- Naagmani Glowing^^

- Naagmani Black
- Sahastra Sampudh Mani^
- Samudrik Mani^^
- Combination of 120-140 Vastu Healing Products to be placed in North-East Direction.
- Gems & Crystals:-
  - Conk Stone^^^
  - Oyester Pearl^^
  - Adra Stone^^
  - Fully Round Natural Pearl^
  - Triphane Gemstone^^
  - Moti Mani^^
  - Yellow Florspar
  - Yellow Spodumene
  - Yellow Beryl
  - Scapolite
  - Samudrik Stone^^
  - Golden Yellow Japanese Coral
- Rudraksha:-
  - 13 Mukhi Rudraksha
  - 18 Mukhi Rudraksha
  - 22 Mukhi Rudraksha^
  - 27 Mukhi Rudraksha
  - 1 Mukhi Trinetra Rudraksha^^
  - 1 Mukhi Jyotir Lingum Rudraksha^^
  - Charam Pashupati Nath Rudraksha

Remedies for Name, Fame & Recognition, To Boost Social Life - Sex Life - Opposite Sex Attraction, To Build Up Reputation, Public Relations (PR) & PAGE-3 Life

In this section, we have provided the right vastu correction tools and vastu dosh nivaran products to be used as remedies for name, fame & recognition, to boost social life - sex life - opposite sex attraction, to build up reputation, public relations (pr) & page-3 life

- Deep Sea Corals *(Specific Patterns Needed)**
- Deep Sea Shells *(Specific Patterns Needed)**
- White Flowers
- Boar Pearl^^^
- Protection Bug Fossil^^^
- Bidaal Mani^^^
- Infinity Gem^^ (Faco Crystal) White
- Kaama Siyar Singhi

- Jungli Kaali Billi ki Jer*^^
- Combination of 120-140 Vastu Healing Products to be placed in South-East Direction.
- Gemstones & Crystals:-
  - Qabana Stone^^
  - White Spodumene
  - Triphane Gemstone^^
  - White Beryl
- Rudrakshas:-
  - 1 Mukhi Trinetra Rudraksha^^
  - 1 Mukhi Jyotir Lingum Rudraksha^^
  - 16 Mukhi Rudraksha
  - 20 Mukhi Rudraksha
  - 25 Mukhi Rudraksha^^

Remedies for Martial Issues, Delay in Marriage, Problems in Love Life, Multiple Affairs, Re-Marriage, Divorce, Seperation, Personal Relations, Relationship Issues.

In this section, we have provided the right vastu correction tools and vastu dosh nivaran products to be used as remedies for martial issues, delay in marriage, problems in love life, multiple affairs, re-marriage, divorce, seperation, personal relations, relationship issues.

- Deep Sea Corals *(Specific Patterns Needed)**
- Deep Sea Shells *(Specific Patterns Needed)**
- White Flowers
- Boar Pearl^^^
- Protection Bug Fossil^^^
- Bidaal Mani^^^
- Infinity Gem^^ (Faco Crystal) White

- Kaama Siyar Singhi
- Siyar Singhi Joda Male Female Pair
- Jungli Kaali Billi ki Jer*^^
- Megha Mani^^
- Moon Rock^
- Aakash Mani Nubh Mani^^
- Bidaal Mani^^^
- Money Eggs^^
- Morogul Mani^
- Samudrik Mani^^
- Conk Pearl Gilabi Mani^^^
- Sahastra Sampudh Mani^
- Combination of 120-140 Vastu Healing Products to be placed in North-West Direction
- Gemstones & Crystals:-
  - Qabana Stone^^
  - White Spodumene
  - Triphane Gemstone^^
  - White Beryl
  - Green Beryl^
  - Parasha Gemstone^^^
  - Samudrik Stone^^
  - Moti Mani^^
  - Oyester Pearl^^
  - Conk Stone^^^
  - Adra Stone^^
  - Fully Round Natural Pearl^
- Rudrakshas:-
  - 1 Mukhi Trinetra Rudraksha^^
  - 1 Mukhi Jyotir Lingum Rudraksha^^
  - 13 Mukhi Rudraksha
  - 15 Mukhi Rudraksha
  - 16 Mukhi Rudraksha
  - 20 Mukhi Rudraksha
  - 21 Mukhi Rudraksha^
  - 22 Mukhi Rudraksha^

> ➢ 25 Mukhi Rudraksha^^
> ➢ 30 Mukhi Rudraksha^^

Remedies for Child Education, Low Energy Levels, Child Growth & Their Overall Personality Development

In this section, we have provided the right vastu correction tools and vastu dosh nivaran products to be used as remedies for child education, low energy levels, child growth & their overall personality development.

- Secret Programmed Vastu Diviner^^ for East
- Specially Formulated Vastu Dosh Nivaran Yantra*^ for East
- Education Tower
- Morogul Mani^
- Sahastra Sampudh Mani^
- Conk Pearl Gilabi Mani^^^
- Infinity Gem^^ (Faco Crystal) Green
- Combination of 120-140 Vastu Healing Products to be placed in East Direction.
- Gems & Crystals:-

- ➢ Conk Stone^^^
- ➢ Oyester Pearl^^
- ➢ Moti Mani^^
- ➢ Orange Beryl
- ➢ Samudrik Stone^^
- Rudrakshas:-
  - ➢ 14 Mukhi Rudraksha
  - ➢ 23 Mukhi Rudraksha

Remedies for Success in Career, Business, Job, Profession, Freelancing, Winning Court Cases & Litigation, Higher Education & Professional Studies

In this section, we have provided the right vastu correction tools and vastu dosh nivaran products to be used as remedies for success in career, business, job, profession, freelancing, winning court cases & litigation, higher education & professional studies.

- Secret Programmed Vastu Diviner^^ for West
- Specially Formulated Vastu Dosh Nivaran Yantra*^ for West
- Morogul Mani^
- Conk Pearl Gilabi Mani^^^
- Infinity Gem^^ (Faco Crystal) Green
- Saam Siyar Singhi
- Jungli Kaali Billi ki Jer*^^
- Gaj Mukta^^^
- Sahastra Sampudh Mani^

- Dhan ka Bandha^
- Samudrik Mani^^
- Combination of 120-140 Vastu Healing Products to be placed in West Direction
- Gemstones & Crystals:-
  - ➢ Oyester Pearl^^
  - ➢ Moti Mani^^
  - ➢ Conk Stone^^^
  - ➢ Kyanite
  - ➢ Cordierite
  - ➢ Samudrik Stone^^
  - ➢ Japanese Blue Coral
  - ➢ Japanese Black Coral
- Rudraksha:-
  - ➢ 19 Mukhi Rudraksha
  - ➢ 28 Mukhi Rudraksha^^
  - ➢ 29 Mukhi Rudraksha^^
  - ➢ 1 Mukhi Trinetra Rudraksha^^
  - ➢ 1 Mukhi Jyotir Lingum Rudraksha^^

Remedies for Mood Swings, Attitude Problems, Misundertsandings, Female Diseases & Gynaecologyical Problems to Females, Confusions in Life, Decision Making, Reputation Among People Around.

In this section, we have provided the right vastu correction tools and vastu dosh nivaran products to be used as remedies for mood swings, attitude problems, misundertsandings, female diseases & gynaecologyical problems to females, confusions in life, decision making, reputation among people around.

- Secret Programmed Vastu Diviner^^ for North-West
- Megha Mani^^
- Moon Rock^
- Aakash Mani Nubh Mani^^
- Infinity Gem^^ (Faco Crystal) White

- Narmadeshwar Shivling White
- Pearl Blisters
- Protection Bug Fossil^^^
- Bidaal Mani^^^
- Siyar Singhi Joda Male Female Pair
- Combination of 120-140 Vastu Healing Products to be placed in North-West Direction
- Gemstones & Crystals:-
  - ➤ Adra Stone^^
  - ➤ Fully Round Natural Pearl^
  - ➤ Triphane Gemstone^^
- Rudraksha:-
  - ➤ 13 Mukhi Rudraksha
  - ➤ 22 Mukhi Rudraksha^
  - ➤ 1 Mukhi Trinetra Rudraksha^^
  - ➤ 1 Mukhi Jyotir Lingum Rudraksha^^

Remedies for Digestion, All Stomach Ailments, Displacement of Naabhi, Immunity & Metabolism Related Issues, Bad Health of Family Members, Long Term Misunderstandings & Family Disputes, Stress & Headaches, Unexpected Losses, Male Dominance, Sudden Accidents & Mishappenings.

In this section, we have provided the right vastu correction tools and vastu dosh nivaran products to be used as remedies for digestion, all stomach ailments, displacement of naabhi, immunity & metabolism related issues, bad health of family members, long term misunderstandings & family disputes, stress & headaches, unexpected losses, male dominance, sudden accidents & mishappenings.

- Antrikha / Space Stone / Space Stone Antrikha^^^
- Infinity Gem^^ (Faco Crystal) White & Green
- Vishnu Chakra Moti^^
- Fully Round Natural Pearl^^

- Tutmak Stone^^
- Timi Stone^^^
- Adra Stone^^
- Enemy Stone^^
- **Conk Stone^^^**
- Qabana Stone^^^
- Protection Bug Fossil^^^
- Eagle Stone^^^
- Triphane Gemstone ^^
- Cordierite^^
- Nagmani Black^
- Naagmani Glowing^^^
- Combination of Kaali Billi ki Jer + Siyar Singhi + Mota Hatha Jodi
- Deep Sea Corals^
- Deep Sea Shells^
- Moon Rock^^
- Natural Pearl Blisters
- Combination of 120-140 Vastu Healing Products to be placed in Brahmasthaana
- Rudraksha:-
  - ➤ 1 Mukhi Rudraksha Gole Dana
  - ➤ 21 Mukhi Rudraksha
  - ➤ Combination of 16 Mukhi Rudraksha + 17 Mukhi Rudraksha + 18 Mukhi Rudraksha
  - ➤ Charam Pashupati Nath Rudraksha
    1 Mukhi Java Rudraksha^^
  - ➤ 1 Mukhi Java Rudraksha Gehuaan Dana^^
- Gemstones: Hiddenite, Parasha, Green Beryl, Yellow Florspar, Yellow Beryl, Yellow Triphane

Remedies for Instability & Fluctuations, Unnecessary Fights Leading to Permanent Damage, Unexpected & Sudden Deaths, Fear & Insecurities, Blood Shed etc.

In this section, we have provided the right vastu correction tools and vastu dosh nivaran products to be used as remedies for instability & fluctuations, unnecessary fights leading to permanent damage, unexpected & sudden deaths, fear & insecurities, blood shed etc.

- Venu Mani^^^
- Raw Burmese Ruby
- Boar Pearl^^^
- Protection Bug Fossil^^^
- Hatha Jodi Actual with Root
- Jungli Kaali Billi ki Jer*^^
- Gaj Mukta^^^
- Jungli Suar ka Daant
- Combination of 120-140 Vastu Healing Products to be placed in South Direction
- Red Gemstones & Crystals:-
  - Qabana Stone^^
  - Wolk Stone^^
  - Heart Shaped Coral
- Rudrakshas:-
  - 17 Mukhi Rudraksha
  - 19 Mukhi Rudraksha^^
  - 26 Mukhi Rudraksha^^
  - 28 Mukhi Rudraksha^^

Remedies for Unknown Problems & Issues, Unexpected Incidents, Negativity, Bad Aura, Black Magic, Evil Eye, Ghostly Activities, Nazar Dosh, Tona-Totka-Tantra Effects, Dominance by Head of the Family or by Outsiders Goes Beyond Tolerance, Administrative Issues, Rahu Bad Effects, Confusions in Life & Bad Decisions etc.

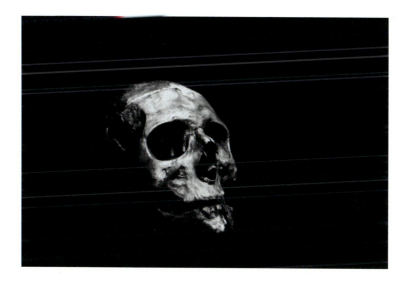

In this section, we have provided the right vastu correction tools and vastu dosh nivaran products to be used as remedies for unknown problems & issues, unexpected incidents, negativity, bad aura, black magic, evil eye, ghostly activities, nazar dosh, tona-totka-tantra effects, dominance by head of the family or by outsiders goes beyond tolerance, administrative issues, rahu bad effects, confusions in life & bad decisions etc.

- Secret Programmed Vastu Diviner^^ for South-West
- Specially Formulated Vastu Dosh Nivaran Yantra*^ for South-West
- Rahu ki Kaudi
- Venu Mani^^^
- Naagmani Glowing^^
- Jungli Kaali Billi ki Jer*^^
- Hatha Jodi Jadh Samet (With Root)
- Brahmajaal
- Protection Bug Fossil^^^
- Boar Pearl^^^
- Talismani Mani for Enemies ^^^
- Antrikha / Space Stone / Space Stone Antrikha^^^
- Gaj Mukta^^^
- Combination of 120-140 Vastu Healing Products to be placed in South West Direction
- Gemstones & Crystals:-
  - Qabana Stone^^
  - Wolk Stone^^
  - Grey Japanese Coral
- Rudrakshas:-
  - 19 Mukhi Rudraksha
  - 28 Mukhi Rudraksha^^
  - 29 Mukhi Rudraksha^^
  - 1 Mukhi Trinetra Rudraksha^^
  - 1 Mukhi Jyotir Lingum Rudraksha^^
  - Charam Pashupati Nath Rudraksha^^^

Part 3

Remedies for Healing North-East Direction

In this section, we have provided the right vastu correction tools and vastu dosh nivaran products to be used as remedies for healing north east direction.

- 9 or 12 Yellow Pyramids
- Yellow Water Pyramid
- Pure Stone Pyramid
- Directional Healing Crystal for North-East
- Secret Programmed Vastu Diviner *^^ for North-East
- Specially Formulated Vastu Dosh Nivaran Yantra for North East *^
- Water Charging Crystals
- Negativity Cleaning Crystals

- Salt Lamp
- Indrajaal
- Protection Bug Fossil^^^
- Morogul Mani^
- Conk Pearl Gilabi Mani^^^
- Yellow Color
- Antrikha / Space Stone / Space Stone Antrikha*^^^
- Nav-Grah Pyramid Yantra
- Naagmani Glowing^^
- Kamakhya Sindhoor
- Sahastra Sampudh Mani^
- Parad Shivling
- Samudrik Mani^^
- Shwetark Ganpati
- Haldi ke Ganesh
- Kastoori
- Gems & Crystals:-
  - Yellow Jade
  - Yellow Aventurine
  - Yellow Jasper
  - Yellow Garnet
  - Conk Stone^^^
  - Deep Yellow Citrine
  - Yellow Triphane Gemstone^^
  - Yellow Tourmaline
  - Yellow Topaz
  - Yellow Opal
  - Oyester Pearl^^
  - Moti Mani^^
  - Yellow Labradorite
  - Yellow Agate
  - Yellow Florspar
  - Yellow Spodumene
  - Yellow Beryl
  - Scapolite

- ➢ Samudrik Stone^^
- ➢ Golden Yellow Japanese Coral
- Rudrakshas:-
  - ➢ 9 Mukhi Rudraksha
  - ➢ 12 Mukhi Rudraksha
  - ➢ 18 Mukhi Rudraksha
  - ➢ 27 Mukhi Rudraksha

Remedies for Healing East Direction

In this section, we have provided the right vastu correction tools and vastu dosh nivaran products to be used as remedies for healing east direction.

- Directional Healing Crystal for East
- Secret Programmed Vastu Diviner^^ for East
- Specially Formulated Vastu Dosh Nivaran Yantra*^ for East
- Education Tower
- Morogul Mani^
- Pure Stone Pyramid
- 5 Orange Pyramids
- Orange Water Pyramid
- Sahastra Sampudh Mani^
- Water Charging Crystals
- Negativity Cleaning Crystals
- Salt Lamp
- Conk Pearl Gilabi Mani^^^
- Orange Color
- Infinity Gem^^ (Faco Crystal) Green
- Sher Ka Daant (Lions Teeth)
- Junglee Suar ka Daant (Wild Pig Teeth)
- Gems & Crystals:-
  - ➢ Orange Sunstone
  - ➢ Orange Topaz
  - ➢ Orange Tourmaline

- ➢ Orange Garnet
- ➢ Orange Opal
- ➢ Conk Stone^^^
- ➢ Orange Sphalerite
- ➢ Orange Flourite
- ➢ Carnelian
- ➢ Oyester Pearl^^
- ➢ Moti Mani^^
- ➢ Orange Agate
- ➢ Peach Aventurine
- ➢ Orange Beryl
- ➢ Orange Citrine
- ➢ Samudrik Stone^^
- ➢ Amber
- Rudrakshas:-
  - ➢ 5 Mukhi Rudraksha
  - ➢ 14 Mukhi Rudraksha
  - ➢ 23 Mukhi Rudraksha

Remedies for Healing South-East Direction

In this section, we have provided the right vastu correction tools and vastu dosh nivaran products to be used as remedies for healing south east direction.

- Directional Healing Crystal for South-East
- Secret Programmed Vastu Diviner*^^ for South-East
- Specially Formulated Vastu Dosh Nivaran Yantra*^ for South-East
- Deep Sea Corals *(Specific Patterns Needed)**
- Deep Sea Shells *(Specific Patterns Needed)**
- Pure & Natural Crystal Balls
- White Flowers
- Boar Pearl^^^
- Protection Bug Fossil^^^

- Negativity Cleaning Crystals
- Salt Lamp
- Bidaal Mani^^^
- Pure Stone Pyramid
- 7 Grey Pyramids
- 925 Sterling Silver Artifacts
- Silver & Sparkling White Colors
- Infinity Gem^^ (Faco Crystal) White
- Kaama Siyar Singhi
- Jungli Kaali Billi ki Jer*^^
- Kamakhaya Sindhoor
- Gemstones & Crystals:-
  - Cubic Zirconia
  - Zircon
  - Asphetic
  - Qabana Stone^^
  - White Topaz
  - White Spodumene
  - Opal
  - Triphane Gemstone^^
  - White Beryl
- Rudrakshas:-
  - 1 Mukhi Trinetra Rudraksha^^
  - 1 Mukhi Jyotir Lingum Rudraksha^^
  - 2 Mukhi Rudraksha
  - 7 Mukhi Rudraksha
  - 16 Mukhi Rudraksha
  - 20 Mukhi Rudraksha
  - 25 Mukhi Rudraksha^^

Remedies for Healing South Direction

In this section, we have provided the right vastu correction tools and vastu dosh nivaran products to be used as remedies for healing south direction.

- Directional Healing Crystal for South
- Secret Programmed Vastu Diviner^^ for South
- Specially Formulated Vastu Dosh Nivaran Yantra*^ for South
- Negativity Cleaning Crystals
- Salt Lamp
- Pure Stone Pyramid
- 8 Red Pyramids *
- Red Color
- Venu Mani^^^
- Raw Burmese Ruby
- Boar Pearl^^^
- Protection Bug Fossil^^^
- Red Lord Hanuman Photo / Idol
- Hatha Jodi Actual with Root
- Jungli Kaali Billi ki Jer*^^
- Kamakhaya Sindhoor
- Shwetark Ganpati
- Gaj Mukta^^^
- Jungli Suar ka Daant
- Dakshinavarti Shankh
- Red Gemstones & Crystals:-
  - ➢ Carnelian
  - ➢ Red Garnet
  - ➢ Qabana Stone^^
  - ➢ Red Jasper
  - ➢ Red Agate
  - ➢ Red Fluorite
  - ➢ Wolk Stone^^
  - ➢ Red Sapphire
  - ➢ Red Spinel
  - ➢ Red Coral
  - ➢ Heart Shaped Coral
- Rudrakshas:-

- ➢ 1 Mukhi Rudraksha
- ➢ 8 Mukhi Rudraksha
- ➢ 17 Mukhi Rudraksha
- ➢ 19 Mukhi Rudraksha^^
- ➢ 26 Mukhi Rudraksha^^
- ➢ 28 Mukhi Rudraksha^^

Remedies for Healing South-West Direction

In this section, we have provided the right vastu correction tools and vastu dosh nivaran products to be used as remedies for healing south west direction.

- Directional Healing Crystal for South-West
- Secret Programmed Vastu Diviner^^ for South-West
- Specially Formulated Vastu Dosh Nivaran Yantra*^ for South-West
- Negativity Cleaning Crystals
- Salt Lamp
- Pure Stone Pyramid
- 10 or 11 Brown Pyramids
- Rahu ki Kaudi
- Venu Mani^^^
- Brown & Grey Colors
- Naagmani Glowing^^
- Jungli Kaali Billi ki Jer*^^
- Hatha Jodi Jadh Samet (With Root)
- Brahmajaal
- Protection Bug Fossil^^^
- Boar Pearl^^^
- Parad Shivling
- Shwetark Ganpati
- Talismani Mani for Enemies
- Antrikha / Space Stone / Space Stone Antrikha^^^

- Sher ka Daant
- Shark Teeth
- Gaj Mukta^^^
- Gemstones & Crystals:-
  - Smokey Quartz
  - Bronzite
  - Brown Agates
  - Grey Agates
  - Qabana Stone^^
  - Tiger's Eye Crystal
  - Amber
  - Wolk Stone^^
  - Smokey Topaz
  - Hessonite Garnet
  - Grey Japanese Coral
- Rudrakshas:-
  - 10 Mukhi Rudraksha
  - 11 Mukhi Rudraksha
  - 19 Mukhi Rudraksha
  - 28 Mukhi Rudraksha^^
  - 29 Mukhi Rudraksha^^
  - 1 Mukhi Trinetra Rudraksha^^
  - 1 Mukhi Jyotir Lingum Rudraksha^^
  - Charam Pashupati Nath Rudraksha^^^

Remedies for Healing West Direction

In this section, we have provided the right vastu correction tools and vastu dosh nivaran products to be used as remedies for healing west direction.

- Blue Water Pyramid
- Directional Healing Crystal for West
- Secret Programmed Vastu Diviner^^ for West
- Specially Formulated Vastu Dosh Nivaran Yantra*^ for West

- Pure Stone Pyramid
- 10 or 11 Black / Blue Pyramids
- Water Charging Crystals
- Negativity Cleaning Crystals
- Salt Lamp
- Morogul Mani^
- Conk Pearl Gilabi Mani^^^
- Education Tower
- Raw Sugilite Crystal
- Raw Turquoise Crystals
- Black & Blue Colors
- Infinity Gem^^ (Faco Crystal) Green
- Narmadeshwar Shivling Black
- Saam Siyar Singhi
- Jungli Kaali Billi ki Jer*^^
- Hatha Jodi
- Gaj Mukta^^^
- Dakshinavarti Shankh
- Sahastra Sampudh Mani^
- Dhan ka Bandha^
- Samudrik Mani^^
- Gemstones & Crystals:-
  - Lapis Lazuli
  - Hematite
  - Angelite
  - Oyester Pearl^^
  - Moti Mani^^
  - Black Obsidian
  - Blue Tourmaline
  - Aquamarine
  - Blue Agate
  - Black Agate
  - Iolite
  - Conk Stone^^^
  - Sodalite
  - Blue Fluorite

> - Blue Amber
> - Azurite
> - Black Opal
> - Black Pearl
> - Black Onyx
> - Black Tourmaline
> - Kyanite
> - Cordierite
> - Samudrik Stone^^
> - Purple Sapphire
> - Japanese Blue Coral
> - Japanese Black Coral
> - Black Spinel

- Rudraksha:-
  > - 10 Mukhi Rudraksha
  > - 11 Mukhi Rudraksha
  > - 19 Mukhi Rudraksha
  > - 28 Mukhi Rudraksha^^
  > - 29 Mukhi Rudraksha^^
  > - 1 Mukhi Trinetra Rudraksha^^
  > - 1 Mukhi Jyotir Lingum Rudraksha^^

Remedies for Healing North-West Direction

In this section, we have provided the right vastu correction tools and vastu dosh nivaran products to be used as remedies for healing north west direction.

- Directional Healing Crystal for North-West
- Secret Programmed Vastu Diviner^^ for North-West
- Negativity Cleaning Crystals
- Salt Lamp
- Megha Mani^^
- Pure Stone Pyramid
- 4 White Pyramids

- Moon Rock^
- Aakash Mani Nubh Mani^^
- Infinity Gem^^ (Faco Crystal) White
- Pearl White Color
- Narmadeshwar Shivling White
- Pearl Blisters
- Protection Bug Fossil^^^
- Bidaal Mani^^^
- Siyar Singhi Joda Male Female Pair
- White Gemstones & Crystals:-
  - Clear Quartz
  - White Agate
  - Adra Stone^^
  - White Jade
  - Fully Round Natural Pearl^
  - Mother of Pearl
  - Moonstone
  - Triphane Gemstone^^
- Rudraksha:-
  - 4 Mukhi Rudraksha
  - 13 Mukhi Rudraksha
  - 22 Mukhi Rudraksha^
  - 1 Mukhi Trinetra Rudraksha^^
  - 1 Mukhi Jyotir Lingum Rudraksha^^

Remedies for Healing North Direction

In this section, we have provided the right vastu correction tools and vastu dosh nivaran products to be used as remedies for healing north direction.

- Green Water Pyramid
- Directional Healing Crystal for North
- Secret Programmed Vastu Diviner^^ for North
- Specially Formulated Vastu Dosh Nivaran Yantra*^ for North

- Water Charging Crystals
- Negativity Cleaning Crystals
- Salt Lamp
- Pure Stone Pyramid
- 3 or 6 Green Pyramids
- Money Eggs^^
- Infinity Gem^^ (Faco Crystal) Green
- Morogul Mani^
- Green Color
- Plants
- Samudrik Mani^^
- Raw Emerald
- Conk Pearl Gilabi Mani^^^
- Indrajaal, Brahmajaal
- Jungli Kaali Billi ki Jer*^^
- Hatha Jodi with Actual Root
- Saam Siyar Singhi
- Sahastra Sampudh Mani^
- Dakshinavarti Shankh
- Dhan ka Bandha*^
- Asphetic Shri Yantra
- Gemstones & Crystals:-
  - Green Jade
  - Conk Stone^^^
  - Green Aventurine
  - Green Agate
  - Green Garnet
  - Green Tourmaline
  - Peridot
  - Hiddenite^
  - Green Amber
  - Green Turquoise
  - Malachite
  - Oyester Pearl^^
  - Moti Mani^^
  - Green Fluorite

- ➢ Green Jasper
- ➢ Amazonite
- ➢ Florite
- ➢ Samudrik Stone^^
- ➢ Parasha Gemstone^^^
- ➢ Green Tourmaline
- ➢ Green Beryl^
- Rudraksha:-
  - ➢ 3 Mukhi Rudraksha
  - ➢ 6 Mukhi Rudraksha
  - ➢ 15 Mukhi Rudraksha
  - ➢ 21 Mukhi Rudraksha^
  - ➢ 25 Mukhi Rudraksha^^
  - ➢ 30 Mukhi Rudraksha^^

Remedies for Healing Bhrahmasthan

In this section, we have provided the right vastu correction tools and vastu dosh nivaran products to be used as remedies for healing brahmasthaana.

- Secret Programmed Vastu Diviner^^ for Brahmasthaan
- Specially Formulated Vastu Dosh Nivaran Yantra^^ for Brahmasthaan
- Kale Ghodhe ki Naal
- Nav-Grah Pyramid Yantra
- Antrikha / Space Stone / Space Stone Antrikha^^^
- Infinity Gem^^ (Faco Crystal) White & Green
- Vishnu Chakra Moti^^
- Combination of 120 Vastu Items & Products
- Fully Round Natural Pearl^^
- Tutmak Stone^^
- Timi Stone^^^
- Adra Stone^^
- Enemy Stone^^

- **Conk Stone^^^**
- Qabana Stone^^^
- Protection Bug Fossil^^^
- Eagle Stone^^^
- Triphane Gemstone ^^
- Cordierite^^
- Nagmani Black^
- Naagmani Glowing^^^
- Combination of Brahmajaal + Indrajaal
- Combination of Kaali Billi ki Jer + Siyar Singhi + Mota Hatha Jodi
- Kamakhaya Sindoor
- Parad Shivling
- Deep Sea Corals^
- Deep Sea Shells^
- Money Eggs^^
- Combination of 120-140 Vastu Healing Products
- Kastoori
- Asphetic Shri Yantra
- Dhan ka Bandha*^
- Moon Rock^^
- Natural Pearl Blisters
- Rudraksha:-
  - 1 Mukhi Rudraksha Gole Dana
  - 21 Mukhi Rudraksha
  - Combination of 16 Mukhi Rudraksha + 17 Mukhi Rudraksha + 18 Mukhi Rudraksha
  - Charam Pashupati Nath Rudraksha
    1 Mukhi Java Rudraksha^^
  - 1 Mukhi Java Rudraksha Gehuaan Dana^^
- Gemstones: Hiddenite, Parasha, Green Beryl, Green Florite, Yellow Florspar, Yellow Beryl, Yellow Spodumene, Scapolite, White Beryl

PART 04

ASTROLOGICAL REMEDIES

In this section, we have provided a list of astrological remedies which can be used for specific directions.

- Yellow Florspar – North-East Direction
- Yellow Spodumene – North-East Direction
- Scapolite – North-East Direction
- Golden Yellow Japanese Coral – North-East Direction
- Orange Beryl – East Direction
- Orange Citrine – East Direction
- Amber – East Direction
- CZ – South-East Direction
- Asphetic – South-East Direction
- White Topaz – South-East Direction
- White Spodumene – South-East Direction
- White Beryl – South-East Direction

- Opal – South-East Direction
- Infinity Gem (Faco Crystal) Green for Studies, Higher Studies, Profession, Career – North Direction, East Direction, West Direction
- Infinity Gem (Faco Crystal) White for Relationships, Marital Relationships, Delay in Marriage – North-West Direction, South-East Direction
- Red Sapphire – South Direction
- Red Spinel – South Direction
- Red Coral – South Direction
- Red Coral Heart Shaped – South Direction
- Smokey Topaz – South-West Direction
- Hessonite – South-West Direction
- Garnet – South-West Direction
- Grey Japanese Coral – South-West Direction
- Kyanite – West Direction
- Cordierite – West Direction
- Purple Sapphire – West Direction
- Natural Pearl – North-west Direction
- Mother of Pearl – North-west Direction
- Florite – North Direction
- Parasha – North Direction
- Green Beryl – North Direction
- Green Tourmaline – North Direction

SPIRITUAL REMEDIES

BLACK CAT'S UMBILICAL CHORD / KAALI BILLI KI NAAL / JUNGLI KAALI BILLI KI JER

It is extremely difficult to procure, but equally useful if preserved. It should be kept in vermillion powder or "sindhoor" in house / mandir or in an office or shop, in a cash box. It is one of the mystic secrets of the orients to get help in the crisis, to improve presence of mind and to raise confidence level. It blesses a person with wealth, prosperity, acquisition and accumulation of money, increasing savings and building assets. It is used for anusthan pratishthaan and particularly for acquisition of wealth.

Traditionally, the billi ki naal is considered as one of the sacred things worth preserving amongst village folks, traders, high profile people, leaders etc. It may not be popular in the cities earlier, but now, every metro resident is also well aware of its miraculous results. One of the reasons of unawareness could be that it is really very difficult to find one. Rarity of the jer or naal makes it an item worth possessing. In the villages families who own it, keep it wrapped in a red cloth or in sindhoor or in a container or tijori. We think that is the best way to keep billi ki jer, which is even good for rahu, mangal and shukra planetary effects.

When a cat gives birth to kittens, she eats her naval chord immediately, which is what makes this item extremely difficult to procure, but equally useful if preserved. Cat's chord should be kept in vermillion powder or 'sindoor' in office, shop or home in a cash box after energizing and activating it properly and performing pran-pratishtha and shuddhi puja. It is commonly used by gamblers, share investors, stock brokers business men, etc. Cat's chord blesses a person with wealth, prosperity, acquisition and accumulation of money, increase in savings and building assets. It is also known as billi ke zer or billi ke jer or billi ki nal. It can solve all karmic problems in a life!

Cat's Umbilical Chord / Billi Ki Naal / Billi Ki Jer is used for South-East, South, South-West, West, North, Bhrahmasthan.

ORIGINAL GIDAR SINGHI URF SIYAR SINGI

Siyar or a jackal, which normally has no horn but when it hoots facing downwards, a small bunch of hair with a horn emerges from his body at the forehead. He sheds it while leaving the herd. This is considered very sacred and known as siyar singhi. It may be of small, medium and big sizes. Having siyar singhi gives immense wealth, victory over enemies, success in litigations and law suits etc.

Siyar singhi is very powerful talisman to remove all sorts of obstacles and black magic from human life having natural powers which transfers to the acquirer directly.

The Brief Description of Siyar Singhi is as Follows: -

One remains fearless of beasts, ghosts and it provides protection, from enemies and evil spirits and gives success in law suits. Siyar singhi shall be kept in vermillion and you have to light up an incense stick in front of him daily or once a week. You will always feel protected when you get this siyar singhi.

'Siyar' is a jackal, and 'singhi' is horns - very rare type of jackals have horns, and these horns are called siyar singhi, gidar singi or siyaar seengh. Siyar singhi should be kept in vermillion powder or 'sindhoor'. Siyar singhi bestows immense wealth, good luck, victory over enemies, and success in ventures, law suits and examinations. It also helps in removing evil spirits, black magic and witchcraft. Siyar singhi has got unusual & strange power which pulls every one-towards itself. Hence it is used by businessmen and shopkeepers to attract customers, generally kept in tijori or their cash box / lockers.

Siyar singhi protects from evil eye, it also helps in removing disembodied spirit. Siyar singhi is the most sought-after lucky charm which is also the rarest.

Gidar Singhi Urf Siyar Singi is used for North, Bhrahmasthan, South-East, West, North-West.

NAAG MANI / NAGMANI / COBRA STONE / SNAKE GEM / SNAKE STONE

Benefits & Its Uses:

Owning such mani is considered good luck, makes person wealthy and fulfill all desires. Possessing a naag mani attains devotion, godliness, good fortune and eventually becomes renowned as a leader of men or masses.

"IT'S THE PERFECT PATH TO SPIRITUAL AWAKENING"

Some facts about the naag mani:

It is said that the size and luster of nag mani increases with the age of the snake. It is moon like pearl stone with Opaque Textured Black Color, and also available in Pale Green / Yellowish Tint which emits light in darkness. But the rarest of them all are the pale green translucent light emitting mani and the other rarest is the one with spiritual fossil textured type pale black opaque ones. They are best among all.

Scientific Facts:
Generally, the life of cobra or king cobra or any snake carrying a naag mani is approx 20 to 30 years in total. It can emit light all night long, but it should get warmth of light or sunrays during the day to emit low fluorescent light in the dark. Generally, snakes and cobras that carry these talismans and manis are found on the asian belt near Himalayas and their river beds, in sri lanka and burma. But most of them are found in the indian subcontinent only.

Generally, the most powerful and rarest of them all emits a pale green light in the dark environments.

Conclusion About Its Reality and Its Existence:

The real naag mani emits pale green light, but there are other types of naag mani which are opaque and doesn't emit light. So, this is not necessary that a translucent mani is only the real one. While the fake nag mani glows only once and then if you change the place there will not be any glow in it. Some fakes keep on glowing continuously in dark. But the real ones absorb light and releases it in the dark. Its glow fades out after it releases all the light it has absorbed.

Some fake naag manis are also identified by such instance - the sellers will take you few feet's away from the place of placement of naag mani and tell you to be silent to show you the magic. Suddenly light starts emitting from the fake mani, it increases slowly. This all operation is done by a far and distance functioning remote in such a way that it reduces the intensity of the light to make you look like it's a real one. It is all an electronic gadget which fools people and innocent believers with all these cheap tricks of fake sellers. Real naag mani is not necessarily complete round and emits light. Some naag mani are smoothened and polished to give the maximum effect to the user. Some of the finest naag manis radiate a natural effulgence and are in pale green color. By repeated washing or polishing, a snake stone or nag mani becomes as lustrous as a polished gemstone.

Anybody who possesses such a snake stone pearl will never be troubled by snakes, devils and spirits, chronic diseases or by any evil or underworld beings.

Naag mani cannot be identified in a gemology lab as it needs special expertise and in-depth knowledge of vedas and granthas to identify the genuineness of a real naag mani. This legend exists in almost all Asian cultures and in well famed the naaga tribe present in India & Tibet.

There are various types of naag mani which may be called stones of a snake or snake stones aka snake gems or snake pearls.

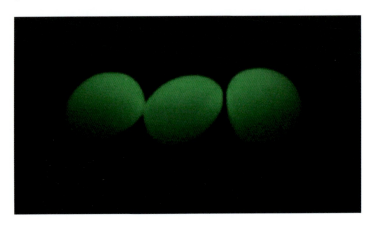

Colors & Power Attributes of Naag Mani:

Naag manis are available in various colors and textures which are either light emitting or glowing ones or the non-light emitting ones. The most valuable and rare ones are pale green in color and spiritually fossilled textured black. These are considered as the most powerful naag manis among all. Others available are yellow, honey orange, red and white in color.

Light Emission and Its Glowing Property:

As far as emission of light is concerned, there are some snake stones or snake pearls which emit light at their own will and some cobra pearl stones do not emit any light at all. The legendary nag-mani shown or most talked about in mythology is just a myth like a big red-light emitting ruby on the hood of the king cobra, which is not available at all, not seen by anybody ever and hence is not available anywhere round the globe. Those are fake naag manis. Lastly, naag manis which are seen are solid and in pale green colour and some are textured black solids. Some are translucent naag manis emitting light, but not up to several feets or meters away, which is just a myth. Real naagmani just glows within or creates a very small aura of its color around. Best ones will glow within itself and are also considered as the most powerfull naag manis available.

After thorough experimentation, it was found that these miraculous talismans emit light or glow in dark and not in lit or lighted environments. One needs to see / place them in dark environments outside on the day of amavasya to see its proper glow as they don't glow much inside the home even in darkest corner of your house.

Naag Mani / Cobra Stone / Snake Gem / Snake Stone is used for North-east, South-West & Bhrahmasthaan.

ORIGINAL HATHA JODI / HATA JORI

Hatha jodi is a type of root that is often described as resembling human arms with clenched fists. Hatha jodi is primarily found in the madhya pradesh area of india, which, according to the national informatics centre, is located in central india and is often called the "heart of india." this plant root grows in this region, as it is rich in large plateaus, large mountain ranges, rivers and miles of dense forests, providing an ideal environment for the plant to flourish.

Powerful Effects
Hatha jodi provides a host of effects, including the ability to hypnotize, shield and improve the financial situation for those who possess it. Its most

274

powerful effect is its shielding effect, as it is said to have protected those who hold it on journeys, in discussions, interviews, and battles by providing the ability to triumph and overcome fear.

Good Luck Charm

Hatha jodi is also considered a rare lucky charm that provides the holder with luck, wisdom, wealth and attractiveness. When the holder is faced with situations in which they are betting, in a trial or need to win favorably, having this root in their possession will encourage their luck and ability to triumph over the other opponent.

Financial Benefits

In addition to providing protection from harm and evil, hatha jodi also offers good luck, wealth and increase in business. It is particularly beneficial for business, as it can help to increase clientele, business status and the attraction power of a person. It does this because it contains the powers of "vashikaran," which is identified in the indian culture as attraction.

Proper Use

While the root is said to contain these powers of promoting bravery, wealth and good fortune, it is important to understand that it can only give these powers if it is properly energised and activated. It must be contained in its pure form, it must always be fresh, and it must be respected. The root is supposed to be washed with water from the ganga river and then placed on a piece of red cloth. Once it is dry, it must be dipped into sindhoor and properly preserved. Finally, it needs to be placed in a devout place where it can be worshiped and respected.

Hatha jodi is a wonder of nature, in which two hands are joined together, as in a prayer. This is actually root of a very rare plant in the shape of folded hands. This, too, should be kept in oil bath because it absorbs oil. Hatha jori blesses the worshipper with wealth and good luck, guards against accidents and bad influences of any tantric effect. It also increases the attraction power of a person, since it has the powers of 'vashikaran' or hypnosis. It is very useful in winning favors or winning trials. Hatha jodi is a plant. It is actually a plant's root with two branches resembling human arms. There is an outline of claw at the end of the arms. The claw in the form of fingers, looks as though it were a human figure who is clenching (tightening) the fists. If both branches of this root are severed and joined together, its shape resembles a clasped hand (folded hand). The plant is mostly found in madhya pradesh. The forest tribes just cut it out / uproot it. Hatha jodi possesses bizarre and providential effects. It is an incarnation of goddess chamunda. It has outstanding powers to beguile, to hypnotize, and to shield people and enhances financial condition.

Hatha jodi shields its worshipper in journeys, discussions, interviews and battle grounds. It furnishes him with triumph. He is no more frightened of supernatural spirits, like ghosts etc. It has proven pretty effective in imparting money and opulence. It holds immense importance in tantrik activities. But hatha jodi is advantageous only when it is pure. A used hatha jodi can be of no advantage to any person. Hence, it must always be fresh.

It is available in all sizes- small and big, but each one is equally efficient. Normally its configuration is the same, as twin arms with folded fingers i.e. The fist.

The Method of Worship

Firstly, one needs to get hold of a hatha jodi. On specific nakshatras it needs to be washed with ganga water in an auspicious yog and then placed on a piece of red cloth. When the water dries up, it should be dipped into sindhoor / vermillion and preserved well. The hatha jodi should be submerged wholly in sindhoor. The pot / bowl needs to be placed in a devout place.

Hatha jori or hatha jodi, is a wonder of nature found in madhya pradesh (india) in amar kantek hills and in the lumibani valley of nepal where there are dark thick forests. Hatha jodi is known as a wonderful tantrik item for influencing people and winning over enemies and clients. It increases the attraction power of a person, since it has the powers of 'vashikaran' or attraction. In these jungles one can find a plant known as ""birvah"" which has blue and white colored flowers and which is similar to the dhatura plant. If one digs carefully on an auspicious occasion / yog / nakshatra, the earth near the roots of this plant will reveal two small sized branches. At that place one will find branches which look like a hand having fingers or those which look like two hands joined together in prayer. This branch is cut and separated, and is called hath jori. Hatha jodi can be small to big in size about 2"-3" to 7" approx. One can see two hands joined together distinctly. This wonder of nature hatha jori shall be kept in vermillon and in silver box or case in puja ghar or locker/almirah. One shall light incense in front of hatha jodi daily. Hatha jodi is great tool for to attract anybody by just keeping in your pocket show amazing results. By just keeping this in your cash box you never run out of money. It gives you abundance of wealth, money and assets.

Hatha Jodi / Hata Jori is used for South, South-West, West, North & Bhrahmasthan.

DHAN KA BAANDHA

This rare occult find is a souvenir in itself. Used mainly for keeping any dwelling, let it be a home or an office, always full of money flow, this rarest treasure delivers it well. It is also used to put in the neeven of the house/office at the beginning of any construction.

Benefits & Uses:
Its placement and presence in particular nakshatras and yogas, whether in a temple, house or office makes the dwelling full of money flow, treasures, wealth, good finances & positivity. Can also be placed in bank lockers, tijori, safe boxes to safeguard your wealth accumulations from evil eyes and theives (protection against theft).

Dhan Ka Baandha is used for healing West, South East & North Directions.

RARE COLLECTION 140 HEALING CRYSTALS IN A STERLING SILVER MALA

This rare spiritual find is a souvenir in itself. It takes lots of guts, patience, time, efforts and money to procure all these crystals, gems and talismans from various countries and sources around the world. Then they are re-sized and customized in almost equal shapes and sizes to make it possible for mounting in a single garland of silver. Then it is energized and activated for best results. All this is a combursome process which takes more than 6 months from the scratch to mounting and energization. Its one of its kind collection among rare talismans. A must for everybody who is spiritual and beleives in natural healing.

Benefits & Uses:

Rarest of the rare. A collection of 121-140 very rare crystals, gemstones and talismani rocks mounted together in a single mala. This rare collection of talismans is used for ultra-healing, spiritual connect, puja archana, clearing bad aura, balancing all chakras specially crown and higher crown chakras, nazar dosh nivaran, balancing body metabolism, removal of evil energies and ghost protection, aura enhancement, deep meditation and spiritual healing, positive energies, protection from evil and ill-health, removal of unwanted bad energies, energy accumulation, cosmic connect, inner strength, godly behavior, image strengthening, public appearances, protection from court cases, enemies & unexpected tragedies, mental stability and presence of mind, godly aura-strength-energy, for wealth-finances and long term stability.

Other Benefits Are:
- Energy Balancing
- Spiritual Connect
- Mass Vashikaran Powers
- Sarva Karya Siddhis
- Akaal Mrityu Suraksha
- Spiritual Protection
- Chakra Balancing
- Karma Yoga
- Personal Relationships
- Huge Monetary & Financial Gains
- Activating Crown N Higher Crown Chakras
- Activating Intuition Powers

- Complete Health Benefits
- Create A Protective Circle Around You
- Great Name & Fame
- Very High Dominance Over The World
- Metal Used: 92.5 Pure Sterling Silver

KAMIYA SINDOOR / KAMAKHYA SINDHUR

Kamiya Sindoor (Specially Formulated Vastu Dosh Nivaran Yantra Vermillion) is also called Kamakhya Sindhur. It is useful for Vashikarn and Winning any court case and getting rid of enemies.

This Siddha Kamakhya Sindoor is beneficial for evil eye, fears, spirit, haunted places and devi (goddess) worship. This Siddha Kamakhya Sindoor is highly charged and energized by shakti mantras and other vedic methods. Kamakhya Sindoor is received from Kamakhya Devi temple at Kaamroo Area in Assam.

It is highly charged already and is used in worshipping of goddess. This is an extremely powerful Sindoor and is basically used by Tantriks. Used it for 41 days and see the magic.

Tradition of wearing sindoor is said to have started 5000 years ago. Female figurines excavated at Mehargarh-Baluchistan, shows that sindhoor was applied to the partition of women's hair even in early Harappan civilization. It is interesting to note that the ancient tradition has still not lost its charm and married ladies still follow it.

Astrological Significance of Sindoor
According to Hindu astrology, Mesh Raashi or the House of Aries is on the forehead. The Lord of Mesh is Mars and the symbolic color is red. It is believed to be very auspicious. That is why red sindoor is applied at the forehead and at the parting of the hair. Both are signs of saubhagya (good fortune). Sindhoor is also considered to be the symbol of the female energy of Parvati and Sati.

Physiological Significance of Sindoor
It is interesting to note that that the application of sindhoor by married women carries physiological significance too. This is so because Sindhoor is prepared by mixing turmeric-lime and the metal mercury. Due to its intrinsic properties, mercury, besides controlling blood pressure also activates sexual drive. This also explains why Sindhoor is prohibited for the widows. For best results,

Sindhoor should be applied right upto the pituitary gland where all our feelings are centered.

Effects, Benefits & Uses of Kamiya Sindhoor

- Increases the body aura level and makes it strong.
- Helps in gaining power for kundlini jagran / awakening
- Enhances the power of third eye.
- Protects from negativity & negative effects of tantra & mantra.
- Builds strong will power.
- Boosts tantra & mantra power.
- Fosters strong and deep meditation.
- Increases the hypnosis power.
- Cultivates healthy husband & wife relationship.

Kamiya Sindoor / Kamakhya Sindhur is used for North-East, South, South-East, Bhrahmasthan.

DAKSHINAVARTI SHANKHA

Dakshinavarti Shankha shows inclination towards the south direction and right side. Though rarely found, it is available in various shades from white to brown with various textures and brown lines on it, which are bleached in the process of cleaning them for sale. Some shankhas comes in spiral and some are not. The prices vary as per the size, texture, color, spiral, gender etc.

Dakshinavarti shankha is a symbol of goddess Maa Lakshmi i.e. the goddess of wealth. Goddess Lakshmi is always portrayed holding a dakshinavarti shankh in her hands. Keeping or placing it at Home, Office, Mandir, Temple, or in Tijori / Cashbox / Locker gives good fortunes, money, lots of wealth, good luck and prosperity.

Dakshinvarti conch or shankhas are very rear to find and their sizes differ from the size of a wheat grain to the size of a coconut-rarest. It drains out all negative energies, purifies the aura and activates positive energies in the atmosphere.

Dakshinavarti Shankha is used for South, West & North.

PARAD SHIVLING

Parad Shivling is made from pure parad / mercury – the most auspicious & pure metal. The Liquid Metal - The only metal found in liquid form and hence the process to bind it or making it solid is very difficult and is done by proper vedic methods and various vidhis prescribed in pauranic granthas and vedic books. It is solidified by using various mixtures of vanaspatis, medicinal herbs according to the Ashta-Sanskaar (the vedic eight methods, which is a very difficult and time-consuming procedure). Its uniqueness stands in its casting and shaping into the lingam.

Mercury or Parad is termed as the sperm / seed of Lord Shiva. In Ayurveda, it as a flowing metalloid or the liquid metal. It is said in Brahma-Purana that whether one is male or a female, Brahmin or a Kshatriya, Vaishya or a Shudra, whosoever worships this Parad Shivling devotedly gets all pleasures of the world & attains salvation or moksha. During their life span they get exaltation, respect, admiration, name and fame, male children, grandsons, knowledge, extra-ordinary powers, superior strength, happiness, peace & prosperity. It is also used many tantric activities, vidhis and pujas.

Mercury has liquid properties which needs proper solidification process to be followed with specific ingredients and timings.

Benefits of Parad Shivlinga :-
- Health, Peace & Prosperity.
- Ample Luxuries & Finances.
- Brings harmony among marital relationships.
- Brings knowledge to the devotee and sharpens memory.
- Used to eliminate the negative effects or the malefic planetary effects of black magic or evil spirits.
- Removes negative impacts of Gau Hatya, Brahm Hatya or Bal-hatya (Ill effects arising due to killing of a cow, a child or a priest).

Parad Shivling is used for North-East, South-West, and Bhrahmasthan.

SHWETARK GANAPATI

Shwetark Ganapati is procured from the root of a flowering shrub that takes the form of Lord Ganesha when carved out of its root, which itself is used as the most sacred and purest form of Shvetark or Aark ki Jad. It is also known as aak or ark ki jar, which is said to have blue and green colored leaves and is found in deep jungles, in mid of Madhya Pradesh.

The possessors of this carved ganpati or the shwetark ganpati in its original root form are blessed with immense wealth and remains free from all evil effects. For doing puja, saadhna and some also practice and do tantric vidhi and tantra saadhna, this root in its purest form is used for the best results. But giving devotion to lord ganesha, it is also carved in its ganpati form and used accordingly. Spiritual connect and lords' blessings are attained by worshipping this shvetark ganpati.

Shwetark Ganapati is used for North-East, South, South-West.

LION'S TEETH / SHER KE DAANT

Well Known for Strength, Power, Flexibility, Fear, Rule, Domination, King Size Lifestyle and Winning Attitude, these Lion's Teeths in Possession let the Possesor Rule the world around. The person using this AMULET Dominates the world and posseses Leadership Qualities. Individuals who are in Politics, Administrative Services, Police Officers, Army Officers, Beaurocrats, Advocates, Lawyers, Judges, Directors, Presidents, Industrialists generally wear / possess this Lion's Teeth to be in power and always remain in power and rule the world around.

Lion's Teeth / Sher ke Daant is used for East, South-West.

INDRA JAL OR MAHA INDRAJAAL

Indra Jal or Maha Indrajaal is a very well-known item in the astrological & religious history of the world. It is a root of a special plant, which is very rarely found & known for its magical effects, if activated properly and be used at your home or office. It is used to get rid of any ill or evil effects, get rid of nazar dosh and financial troubles, black magic, vastu dosh nivaran, clear out the negative energies around, activate the positive energies, guard the place against theft, and activate luck of the occupants. For immediate results & faster relief, it should be placed well or as prescribed by a professional. In scientific language, it is known as Sea Fan.

Its also very much helpful in peace of mind and harmony in family. It helps in financial crisis and makes a person intelligent. Its a unique item to overcome the enmity, sickness, loss in business etc. It also brings money and power.

It protects the adversity and help to overcome unnecessary harassment and loss of prestige. great tool for vastu dosh nivaran, a very rare tantrik product.

Indrajaal is very rare and of great importance. It can not be found easily and can not be imitated easily. Its importance and benefits are mentioned in scriptures like Dawaratantra, Vishwasara & Ravan Sanhita. It gives great benefits to a person if he keeps it in his place of worship / puja ghar or in your living room or getting it framed and mounted on wall. It is also considered as talisman, full of positive energies and magical powers.

Indra Jal or Maha Indrajaal is used for North-East, North, Bhrahmasthan.

GARUDA MANI | EAGLE STONE | EAGLE PEARL | GARUD MOTI | GARUD MANI | GARUDA MOTI

GARUDA MANI Charaterstics, Features & Benefits: Winning Over Court Cases, Develop hunting & preying skills, Gives keen power of observation, Wide reach in terms of popularity, It gives a never to surrender attitude, It will let you regain your lost territory, Gives ability to work together in groups, It gives complete dominance over others, It always gives a fight to win over enemies, Makes you a fearless and successful leader, It gives you ability to strategize and plan well, Possessing this is equivalent to touching face of god, Gives you an eagle eye to minutely study and observe, Makes you more focused, gives clarity over your thoughts, It makes one check and balances of his personal and professional lives, It gives ability to face Challenges in the life like great leaders and to rise to greater heights, It gives you strong Vision. Vision is a successful leadership, characteristic, which is seen in all the great leaders of this world. It enhances Courage, pride, bravery, honor, grace and determination, makes you more social and active. It is symbolic to transcendence, soaring high, freedom and power.

It is used for Hypnotism, vashikaran, it improves the financial situation, gives shielding effect, overcomes fear, gives luck, wisdom, wealth and attractiveness, provides protection from harm and evil effects, offers good luck, wealth and increase in business, beneficial for business, as it can help to increase clientele, business status and the attraction power of a person. It also contains vashikaran powers, blesses the worshiper with wealth and good luck, it's a lucky charm, guards against accidents and bad influences of any tantric effect. It also increases the attraction power of a person, since it has the powers of 'Vashikaran' or Hypnosis. It is very useful in winning favours or winning trials.

Garuda Mani is used for North, North West, South, South West & Bhrahmasthan.

NAVA MANI

<u>Nava Mani</u> - Oyster Pearl, Conch Pearl, Cobra Pearl, Boar Pearl, Elephant Pearl, Bamboo Pearl, Whale Pearl, Fish Pearl, Cloud Pearl

Nava Mani, The Nine Pearls, The Nine Vedic Pearls or The 9 Vedic Pearls is what we call as the Nava Moti, or the Nine Gems or Nau Mani. In Garudra Puran, these 9 gems are described as a group of sacred gems in its vedic text. These Nava Moti or Nava Mani are as follows:

CLOUD PEARL
WHALE PEARL
ELEPHANT PEARL (GAJ MUKTA)
COBRA PEARL (NAAG MANI)
OYSTER PEARL
FISH PEARL
BAMBOO PEARL
BOAR PEARL
CONCH PEARL

Though most of the pearls are most difficult to procure and are not found these days, but some of them are still available in the international market. The available pearls out of these nava mani are Elephant Pearl (Gaj Mukta) & Cobra Pearl (Naag Mani).

CLOUD PEARL | MEGHA MANI

Also Called Mega Mani or Megha Mani. These are very rare and big in size. Though various sizes are available in this mani, but most of them are dark blue to light blue in color. Some are having spirals around. And some are having just shades of blue around them. Mostly mix textures of blue and various other colors have also be seen in these cloud pearls, which can still be found. These gems are translucent to opaque in color.

These cloud pearls rarely reaches the ground. Generally, these pearls are found with either gem collectors, antique collectors, or with the age-old hierarchy of kings and their heirs, who have started selling them now for good fortunes as their kingdom and old royal days have gone now. Sea sailors and fish catchers have been seen with these types of gems, most often, selling them in the international markets for some instant fortune.

It is said that these pearls or megha manis are formed in the clouds, in the 7th layer of the wind of the sky, and when the lightening strikes. It reaches earth during a big cloud burst or when the lightening strikes through the clouds. It is generally found deep in the soft sand of the unexplored sea shores and islands lost deep in the sea. Lighting strikes and water waves are another source of carrier for these gems or cloud pearls.

WHALE PEARL | TIMI MANI | JUMBU MATSYA MANI

Whale Pearls or Jumbu Matsya Mani are generally big round rough textured stones found in various colors. With vague patterns seen in some of these gems, there is no a huge probability of having them in various textures, sizes and colors. Some are translucent and some appears to be opaque in color. But transparent variety is never seen. The most VALUABLE among all are the opaque round shaped deep yellow or light to dark golden color whale pearls with some moon surface like small dents on it. White to yellow tints and shades and odd round shapes are also seen sometimes. These arc said to be found in the mouth of whales, which they throw out after a certain period and sailors collect them as treasures in the deep blue sea and high waters.

Sometimes they resemble a fish's eye as well. These pearls are known to be very sacred, pure, powerful and valuable. These pearls said to have innumerable powers and they posses a heavenly energy to gain power and wealth. These are priceless gems as there is no fixed price set for these talismans.

ELEPHANT PEARL | GAJA MANI | GAJ MUKTA

These pearls or gaj mukta is said to be found in the temple of a special species of elephants and old mammoths thousands of years old. Those pearls are big rock or brick like structures with odd shapes having sheen or dull lustre over it. These are collected from the fossils of those elephants and being auctioned at the international auction houses. Then these are cut and polished in pieces to make it more wearable and usable.

The pearls are usually formed in the head and in the tusk sockets of these Airavata Elephants, which are not present today. The size of a pearl or gaj mukta is very large, huge and in various odd shapes. These are worn by kings in various forms of jewellery like rings, bracelets, carved necklaces etc. For more info and its benefits, click here.

COBRA PEARL | NAAG MANI | NAGAMANI

These are the miraculous gems, found in deep jungles, where snakes do hunting at night. These pearls are either opaque black in color with special texture over it Or are available in dull pale greenish color, which has a property to absorb light and emit light for a specific duration, depending upon its size, in the dark environments. It is this property of emitting light at dark in the night is what snakes use to lure its prey from far distance. Cobra snakes put it on the grass near their mouth and stay calm, hide in the grass or behind leaves. This camouflage them from the eyes of the birds and large dragon flies, which gets attracted to the light of naag mani. The glowing nagmani attracts the prey for the snake and they hunt them easily without putting in much of the effort. Snake charmers pick these mani by tricking the snakes and cobras.

Naagamani, also called nagamani, serpent stone, snake stone, serpent pearl and cobra stone is said to give good fortune to its possessor, its a king maker stone, protects you from unexpected happenings and chronic diseases. It gives immense wealth and great health to the owner of this talismani mani. For more info and its benefits, click here.

CONK PEARLS | GILABI MANI

A Gilabi Mani comes from a rare species of greater conch family, where it is rarely formed. Though it is formed in the digestive tract, but colors variate a lot depending upon the rarity. Some are very rare colors, that's why they are very expensive like deep pink, golden yellow, red, reddish white pinkish white tench, but it can variate and comes in vast variety of shades like white, pale while, dull white to pale yellow, creamish and off-white yellow shades. Though shapes variate sometimes, these are polished to make them more oval or round so that Vastu & External Dimensions are in proportion to make it more valuable, wearable, soothing to eyes and to give best possible healing. An intestinal deposit in the conk is what makes it more valuable and rarer. It cannot be cultivated or grown artificially in any lab. It is all naturally found and is categorized as a bezoar stone as well.

It is not nacre, that's why it is devoid of its color, luster and brilliancy. But as far as AUSPICIOUS & HEALING POWERS are concerned, out of all 8 species of the Pearls found worldwide, Gilabi Moti & Gaja Moti (Gaj Mukta or Elephant Pearl) found in the temple of elephants are the most precious, valuable, powerful and treasured among all pearls. It is seen in various sizes differentiating in small, medium and large. Though larger sizes are rarer and more difficult to find. These are priceless treasures, as there is no specific price or cost set for them.

FISH PEARL | MATSYA MANI

Fish Pearls or Matsya Mani are found in the mouth or stomach of a fish. It is not found in every fish. Very few fish carry this talisman.

Matsya Mani are rough to plain textured variated pattern formations, found in various sizes from very very small to very large stones. They are found in translucent to opaque form. These fish pearls are generally white in color with various shades on it ranging from pink to yellow to light green to blue tints. These are priceless talismans found with fishermen and sea sailors, who sell them to collectors and traders. There is no fix price set for these treasures as they differ as per the rarity, color and textures.

BAMBOO PEARL | VENU MANI

Mostly round in shape, but sometimes come in different uneven round shapes also. small to big balls shaped, colors ranging from off white to brownish earthy woody mix shades, flat and sometimes uneven, have light texture like a rough mix wood, as these are found in the hollow stem of bamboos. These Bamboo Stem Pearls generally do not have any lustre or flaw in the skin. Mix shades ranging from white to dark brown suffixes the flaws and its texture behind it. But its a rare natural occurrence. That's why there is no specific price set for these treasures.

These are extremely precious possessions, rare and valuable, objects of desire possessed by kings from centuries, gives name, fame, wealth, gives healing to chronic diseases and cures them, cures grief and sorrow, and blesses childless couples with sons.

BOAR PEARL

Generally, Boar Head Pearls are found in round to oval to egg like shapes, dark in color, opaque with most rough texture around. But they can be polished and smoothed on demand. They are found in the temples and head area of wild boars. Mostly found in the specific areas and digging sites of the world, natives collect them while they dig for archaeological or construction purposes and sell them.

It gives divine strength, overall healing, win over enemies, sexual power and strength, high intuition powers, gives good luck, stability and progress in business, job & profession, attraction for opposite sex, high personal charisma, peace, harmony and great social standing. These are priceless possessions with no specific price set for these treasures.

OYSTER PEARL | MOTI MANI | CHANDRA MANI | MOON'S GEM

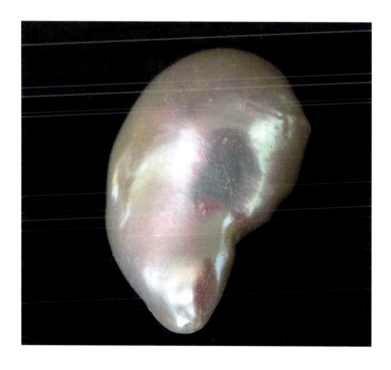

Though Oysters are used in spells for banishment, wealth and divine opulence, but they are more known for their pearl generating capabilities. Oysters generally protect themselves from the irritating grains of sand. In order to protect itself, it quickly start covering the grain of sand with a mineral substance called layers of nacrc. When oyster starts covering it with layers and layers of nacre on the sand grain, also called as mother of pearl, it creates a gem called Pearl or Oyster Pearl.

These Pearls are flawless textured round ball shaped pieces of treasure. Also found with dents on it in various sizes ranging from very small to very large sizes measured in carats. Perfect round ones with no dent or pot hole are the most precious ones. Japanese oyster pearls are the best among them all.

PAARAS BOOTI

Uses & Effects

Extreme Business Growth & Expansion | High Income & Career Growth | Extreme Riches & Wealth Collection | Deep Bond & Love Relationships | Activating Sixth Sense & Love Life | Activating Strong Intuition Powers

Other Features, Testing & Benefits of Paras Booti / Paaras Buti

#. Its a Rarest of the Rare "Talisman"

#. Its a HIGH POWERED Natural Booti

#. Very Fast & Extreme Results

#. Winning Court Cases Against Enemies

#. Moves in Water or When Touched by Water

#. Good for High Business Growth & Expansion

#. Used for High Income & Career Growth

#. Overseas Connections & Corporate Alliances

#. Good for Married Couples, Marital Bond & Love

#. Good for Love Marriages / Delay in Marriage

#. Used to Get Desired Life Partner

#. Good for Social Tie-Ups & Public Relations

#. Used for Strengthening Personal Relations

#. Used for Strengthening Family Relations

#. Used for High Intuitive Powers & Activating Sixth Sense

Paaras Booti is used for North, North East, East, West & Bhrahmasthan.

GAJ MUKTA | GAJA MUKTA | GAJA MANI | ELEPHANT PEARL | ELEPHANT STONE | ELEPHANT HEAD PEARL | HAATHA MANI | HATHI MANI | HATHA MOTI | HAATHI MOTI | GAJ MANI | GAJ MOTI

Benefits, Uses & Effects Of Gaj Mukta

Make one feel like a king, Gives Immense Riches, Money and Wealth, Removes all Black Magic & Jaadu Tona Effects, Removes All Curses of Previous Birth & Badd Dua, It keeps away stress, bad aura and negativity around, Make you feel like KINGS with dominance over the world, Can make you Win Court Cases with Guaranteed Results, Owned by Kings and Maharajas of old times, giving high riches, Can CURE very Acute and Chronic Diseases, without any side effects, Used to Gain & Accumulate Wealth, Name, Fame, Good Luck & High Fortunes, Used for Happy MARRIED Life & Gives Immense Dominance & Leadership Qualities, Can CURE Diseases like Cancer, Childlessness, Progeny, Impotency, Joint Pains, Arthritis etc.

A Gajmukta is a white to pale yellow ivorish color oval anatomical structure with light texture and a dull sheen on it. It has some great therapeutic uses, medicinal properties and some strange and magical healing powers. It can even cure cancer and other chronic ailments. Its like a white ivorish pearl found in very few species of elephants. It's a natural and antique article, extremely rare to find and very expensive. Has some great benefits like bringing huge fortune to the owner of this elephant pearl and these are also considered as some priceless treasures and rare finds found in certain type of elephants in the deep jungles in ancient times.

Truth Behind Its Functions And Myths Behind It
Though being very expensive, there are so many myths attached with this article. Some of them are very well known like a Paan ka Patta / Beatle leaf wrapped around and it gets eaten up by gajmukta, like clean water turns milky after being touched by it, like feeling of heartbeat in it as if it is alive (ha ha ha), like coconut water and bubbles, like it drinks and absorbs water etc. etc. etc. Let me clear out one thing very

profoundly. These are all myths and one has created it and others had copied, pasted and followed it blindly. But in my community of more than 900 saints, pandits, gurus, spiritual gurus, karm kaandis, purohits, tantrics and occult practioners, antique collectors and occult dealers, whom I met personally or talked from worldwide in my very big career, Nobody Has Ever Seen or Felt Any of These Effects In Any Gajmuktas available worldwide. These mythologies are used to fool innocent people about it and after selling nothing works.

True Function and How To Test Gajmukta!
Real Gaj Mukta has a dull sheen of an ivory and sheen of a pearl mixed together. That's why it is called Elephant Pearl. Its construction is based on the collective elements inside the Head, Bone Marrow, Calcium, Vitamin D, the fluid of the head of the elephant and a strange secretion of a fluid inside the brain of the elephant which goes to this pearl and hence it is created. Its exclusive formation and existence is said to be evaluated from the calcified masses collectively inside the head of the elephant. That is why it is also called as Gaja Mani and is a rare find.

Most of the ancient elephants has a tendency to create this type of Pearl inside, but generally the process gets started and ends very fast, which results in either dissolving the mani or gajmukta or it doesn't takes its form ever. Sometimes small gajmuktas are formed due to this fast ending process. But some of the types and species of ancient elephants believed to be known as Airavata Species has this tendency to create this elephant pearl / gajmukta / haathi mani inside their head. During the creation, it takes months, sometimes years and some elephants even gets weaker physically in that process of creation. So to test this mani, one should sit in NE direction with mani in the right hand, close the palm, meditate, there should not be any disturbance around and concentrate specifically on gaja mani in your right hand with closed eyes. Once closed, you should not open your eyes till 90 minutes atleast. If your crown chakra and higher crown chakra are open, clear and clean, then you will feel sudden vibrations in your hand / body / head. These vibrations can be very subtle, slow, low when your third eye is not opened up. But if you are spiritually connected, then you may feel very high vibrations, high heart beat levels, a severe pain in the heart / neck / spinal cord, right hand/arm, hard pain in the head or back of the head. Some have even felt a sudden very high voltage jolt / shock and they have opened their eyes immediately. This is how you test gaj mukta as it takes all your energy of the body and re-channelize it, then give it back to you with a back force. And actually, that is what its primary function is – "TO HEAL PHYSICAL BEING, YOUR BODY AND SOUL"

Its Importance, Benefits, Scientific Relevance and Mythological Connections

The most important aspects and its benefits are

mentioned here about this most valuable, magical and divine gajmukta. The main characterstics are:

Gives Immense Riches, Money and Wealth, Removes all Black Magic & Jaadu Tona Effects, Removes All Curses of Previous Birth & Badd Dua, It keeps away stress, bad aura and negativity around, Make you feel like KINGS with dominance over the world, Can make you Win All Court Cases with Guaranteed Results, Owned by Kings and Maharajas of old times giving High Riches, Can CURE very Acute and Chronic Diseases, & has very Soothing Effects, Used to Gain & Accumulate Wealth, Name, Fame, Good Luck & High Fortunes, Used for Happy MARRIED Life & Gives Immense Dominance & Leadership Qualities, Can cure diseases like Cancer, childlessness, progeny, impotency, joint pains, arthritis etc.

It is a tool used for spiritual and physical healing from ages. Heals your chakras, and mind, a silent healer, gives peace and harmony and has high level of vibrations. It has very subtle radiations of a natural pearl as well.

Gaj Muktas have been given many names. It is available as Male or Female, but various other names only leads to 2 differentiators as male and a female only. People do call it by different names, like Supradika Gaja Mani or Elephant Kiwifruit, Pushpadanta Gaja Mukta or Elephant Mukta, Airavata Gaja Mani, Kumuda Gaja Mani or Elephant Gem, Sarvabhauma Gaja Mani or Ingenious Elephant, Pundarika Gaja Mani or Elephant bezoar, Anchana

Gaja Mani or Elephant Geliga, Vamanan Gaja Mani or Elephant Mustika, Thamrakarni, Abhramu Gaja Mani, Subhra-danti elepant Pearl, Anupama Gaja Mani, Angana elephant bezoar, Pingala Gaja Mani, Anjanavathi Elephant Stone, Kapil Gaja Mani etc. etc. But mainly it bifurcates into 2 available forms, either as a Male Gajmukta or a Female Gajmukta.

It is said to give all kinds of wealth to its possessor, cures incurable diseases, victory over the world, and neutralize sins. The best way to test / know about the real and genuine Gaja Mukta is that it looks like a dull ivory with a pale light yellowish tint and light texture patterns.

Gaja Mukta is used for North West, South East, South West, South & Bhrahmasthan.

PAASHA JAAL

Healing Properties of PASHA JAAL

It Reverse the Black Magic Done on You | Removes Bad & ill Effects of Black Magic & Goes Back to the Sender | Creates a Protective Shield Around You | Removes all Types of Black Magic, Vodoo, Kaala Jaadu, Sufi Tantra, Muslim Tantra, Bengali Tantra, American & African Magic, Chinese Magic, Japanese Magic, White Magic, WitchCrafts etc & Cleanses Your Body | Nullifies & Neutralizes Any Magic & Tantra Done on You!

"CREATES A PROTECTIVE PAASHA JAAL AROUND YOU"

Business, Money, Name, Fame, Finance, Good Job, Business Growth, to get rid of Hidden Enemies &

Competitors, Winning Over COURT CASES, Cure Hidden Diseases-Health Issues & Unknown Black Magic-Jaadu Tona, Vashikaran, Sex, Vitality, Love Life, Good Relationships, Youth, Sexual Power, Attracting Opposite Sex etc.

Other Benefits Are As Follows:
It attracts the magic and luck, Provides safety from the hidden enemies, Helps in soul retrieval, Creates a protective shield around your spiritual aura, It activates and enhances intuition, intellect & insight, Good for Hidden motivations, Correcting emotion imbalances & behaviors, Gives Immense, Spiritual Support, Activates Higher State of consciousness, Initiates deep inner voyages, Supports Silver Spirits & Angels, Opens & Activates Third Eye Chakra, Activates Crown Chakra & Root Chakra, Great Talisman used for Gazing Purposes, Controls aggression & anger, Concentration towards his focus, Stone used to Enhance Luck, Supports shamanistic vibrations, Stimulates deep intuition, It clears the psychic visions, It evokes the soul experience, It protects from deceitful entities, It blends earthy energy with yin & yang, It Communicates with natural elementals, Aids spirituality & creates strong elemental energy, Created a peaceful & calm shield around the wearer, Connects your heart with your brain & creates a great balance, To Know your inner self & self realization of your inner powers, Works as a bridge to connect between the physical & natural world, Activates Godly energies in your aura &

Absorbs them from the surroundings, Cures various Diseases like diabetes, pneumonia, skin infections, lung diseases, Lung Blockage, Lung Cancer, Lung Issues, Lung Clearance of its Walls, insulin regulation, skin inflammation etc.

TALISMANI MANI FOR WEALTH, FINANCES, MONEY

Talismani Mani is used for Various Purposes like:
Sudden Financial Gains, Higher Profits, Higher Money Inflow, Good Luck in Shares & Stock Market, Unexpected Wealth, Riches & Monetary Gains, Getting Favors from Government & High Class

Officers, Govt. Officials, Used for Commercial Success & Profits from Long Term Investments, Will instantly activate your Profitability & your Luck for Monetary Gains & for Accumulating Huge Wealth, Winning Lottery, For Match Fixing, For Gambling Purposes, For Winning in Casino & Roulette Games, Winning in Horse Race, To Win in Betting & with Bookies etc.

Paasha Jaal is used for North West, South East, South West, South, West & Bhrahmasthan.

REMEDIAL RUDRAKSHAS

One Mukhi (Face) Rudraksha

Rudraksha of a single face is Laxmi Rupam. The possessor of this invaluable and rarest rudraksha shall be surrounded with tremendous wealth. Will enjoy peak respect and reputation, never face domination, face no danger, remain free from worries, will not die of sudden death. One Mukhi is used for South Direction & for Bhrahmasthan.

Two Mukhi (Face) Rudraksha

A rudraksha of two faces is shiva and parvati rupam. One that possesses this rudraksha shall always attain complete mental peace. It has the rare radiation power to keep the mind balanced and cool, even in crises. It is highly useful to thinkers, debaters, judges, lawyers, saints and sages, scientists and research scholars. Two Mukhi Rudraksha is used for South-East Direction.

Three Mukhi (Face) Rudraksha

A rudraksha of three faces is lord masaraswoti roopam. This rudraksha is immensely useful to those who attract frequent illness of one kind or the other. It is also useful to those who are generally physically weak. It is highly useful to the victims of jaundice. It is helpful to the job and employment seekers. Three Mukhi Rudraksha is used for North Direction.

Four Mukhi (Face) Rudraksha

Brahma roopam, four face rudraksha is good for meditation. It is considered useful to those have dull mind, are inactive slow and sluggish. Its radiation influences spirit to those who are unimpressive in their talk and conversation and speech. It helps in elevating the depressive personality. Four Mukhi Rudraksha is used for North-West Direction.

Five Mukhi (Face) Rudraksha

A rudraksha of five face is rudra himself i.e. pancheswor roopam.it contact in the body destroy five lopas - kama (lust), Lopa (greed), Mooha (too much attachment), Krodha (jealousy), Ahancar (unwanted ego). It is very good for those having heart diseases, blood pressure, stress etc. Five Mukhi Rudraksha is used for East Direction.

Six Mukhi (Face) Rudraksha

A rudraksha with six faces is karthikean roopam. It brings all sorts of enjoyment in women. This should be were in the left hand by the meditating om namaha shivaya namaha. Those who want to prevent evil strength towards them are beneficial from this rudraksha. Six Mukhi Rudraksha is used for North Direction.

Seven Mukhi (Face) Rudraksha

A rudraksha of seven faces is saptarishi roopam. Wearing this rudraksha is good for those who are in business as well as in share and gambling business. Even holding it, a poor man becomes a great achiever of prosperity in life. Diseases like asthma, respiratory diseases as well as disease of thorax are prevented. Seven Mukhi Rudraksha is used for South-East Direction.

Eight Mukhi (Face) Rudraksha

Rudraksha of eight faces is called ganesh roopam. Before doing any new work, its contact or vision improves and bring good fortune of future work. After death he or she becomes the trident bearing lord shiva. Diseases of stomach are prevented by wearing this rudraksha. Eight Mukhi Rudraksha is used for South Direction.

Nine Mukhi (Face) Rudraksha

A rudraksha of nine faces is navadurga roopam. It is good for body strength. Wearing it in the body stimulate the nine hormone or rasa which improves the will power of the wearer. This rudraksha shall be worn on the left hand with great devotion. Nine Mukhi Rudraksha is used for North-East Direction.

Ten Mukhi (Face) Rudraksha

A rudraksha of ten faces is vishnu roopam. It is good for those who seek mukti in life. Wearing it, the devotees shall achieve fulfillment of all desire. Diseases like hormonal imbalance in the body, thought in-coordination, etc. are removed even by looking it.

Ten Mukhi Rudraksha is used for West Direction.

Eleven Mukhi (Face) Rudraksha

It represents the eleven roopam of lord shiva (akads rudra), by wearing it one becomes victorious everywhere. It is good for the willpower; lengthen the life of human with complete happy life. Diseases like body pain, backache, chronic alcoholism, liver diseases are prevented. Eleven Mukhi Rudraksha is used for West Direction.

Twelve Mukhi (Face) Rudraksha

A rudraksha of twelve faces is sulpani roopam (god sun). It is good for the politician and people who look for much better position in society. Diseases like bone diseases, rickets, osteoporosis etc. are removed as it help in the absorption of light from the sun. All the twelve aditays are present in this rudraksha, which make person more powerful and famous. Twelve Mukhi Rudraksha is used for North-East Direction.

Thirteen Mukhi (Face) Rudraksha

A rudraksha of thirteen faces is viswadeva (indra), wearing it man will attend the realization of all desire. He will derive good future and auspiciousness. It makes man to tame other people and animals. Diseases of muscle like dystrophies, etc. will be removed. The man wearing it will remain attain servaguna of life. Thirteen Mukhi Rudraksha is used for North-West Direction.

Fourteen Mukhi (Face) Rudraksha

A rudraksha of fourteen faces is lord parmatma shiva roopam. It makes the man more kindness to the living things and become superior in the society. He will be very near to shiva and feel his breath with omkar vibration. Wearing it prevents all sorts of diseases in the human body as well as never suffers from any disastrous situation. Fourteen Mukhi Rudraksha is used for East Direction.

Fifteen Mukhi (Face) Rudraksha

A rudraksha of fifteen faces is lord pashupatinath. Those people who has done wrong thing in their life knowingly or unknowingly will be removed. Rudraksha of fifteen faces will attract all the intellectual power. Rudraksha of fifteen faces is very helpful for women from the diseases like still birth, repeated miscarriage etc.

Health, wealth, power, energy, prosperity, elevation of soul and increase in spiritual power. Blesses one with true happiness and inner peace, leads one to the right path, and improves 'karma', destiny and future. Fifteen Mukhi Rudraksha is used for North Direction.

Sixteen Mukhi (Face) Rudraksha

A rudraksha of sixteen faces is hari-shankar roopam. It represents the combine forms of vishnu and shiva. It is good for those who are sick for affection from other in the family. Diseases like leprosy, tuberculosis and the lung diseases are prevented by wearing this rudraksha. The house in which it is kept is free from fire, theft or robbery. It represents the victory and the possessor is never affected by heat or cold. It especially useful for the saints living in jungles. The house in which it is kept is free from fire, theft or robbery. Sixteen Mukhi Rudraksha is used for South-East Direction & for Bhrahmasthan.

Seventeen Mukhi (Face) Rudraksha

A rudraksha of seventeen faces is sita-rama roopam. It is good for success in all desire of life. Wearing this rudraksha, kundalini can be awakened. Even seeing it or contact improves the memory of human being and works for deserving life. Diseases like lack of memory, inability to do hard works are prevented. It is very effective in gaining the unexpected money. It is especially useful in attaining the property, vehicles and all physical assets. It represents the victory and the possessor is never affected by heat or cold. The house in which it is kept is free from fire, theft or robbery. Seventeen Mukhi Rudraksha is used for South Direction & for Bhrahmasthan.

Eighteen Mukhi (Face) Rudraksha

A rudraksha of eighteen faces is bhairava roopam. It is terrible form of lord shiva. Wearing it remove the bad effect coming to the body. Wearer is freed from the fear of death. The possessor is blessed with all kinds of fame, respect and success related to spiritual progress. It prevents the human being from most of the accident as well as form enemy. Diseases like mental incoordination, loss of power are removed. It represents the mother earth. The possessor remains happy and healthy. It is especially beneficial for the pregnant women in protecting their child.

THE GREAT BIBLE OF "REMEDIAL VASTU"

Eighteen Mukhi Rudraksha is used for North-East Direction.

Eighteen Mukhi Rudraksha is used for Bhrahmasthan.

Nineteen Mukhi (Face) Rudraksha

A rudraksha of nineteen faces narayan roopam. Worshiping it or wearing gives victory of true and knowledge over ignorance and demon activity. The possessor is bestowed with all worldly pleasures. There is no scarcity in their life. Diseases like blood disorder, spinal disorder are prevented. It represents lord narayana. The possessor is bestowed with all worldly pleasures. There is no scarcity in their life. Nineteen Mukhi Rudraksha is used for South-West & West Direction.

Twenty Mukhi (Face) Rudraksha

A rudraksha of twenty faces is janardana roopam. Wearing it, the devil, nicked planets, ghost and spirit hunting around funeral places etc. will not come near to him. The possessor is bestowed with continuous progress in his divine faith and spiritual knowledge. Diseases like snake bites is cured by wearing or holding the rudraksha. Twenty Mukhi Rudraksha is used for South-East Direction.

Twenty-One Mukhi (Face) Rudraksha

A rudraksha of twenty-one face is lord shiva. By wearing this remission from the sins of bramahatya could be procured. Moreover wearing it or worshiping it in the house stabilizes the entire environment and relationship of human to soul. The man holds this rudraksha is never down on his achievement. All gods reside within the surrounding of this rudraksha where it is placed for worship. Wealth and health always remain within the family possessing this rudraksha. The bearer will famous for prosperity and spirituality and always remains in the path of sanatan dharma. It is helpful in opening the third eye chakra which governs clairvoyance, sharpened skills, heightened state of awareness etc. Twenty-One Mukhi Rudraksha is used for North-Direction & for Bhrahmasthan.

Gauri Shankar Rudraksha

A rudraksha of gauri shankar is shiva parvati roopam. Goods for reunification in all sorts of life problems. It helps in good attachment of family in all respects. Worshiping gauri shankar, the pain and suffering and other earthly obstacles are destroyed and the peace and pleasure of family are increased. Diseases like sexual problems, detachment and behavioral disorders are removed. Gauri Shankar Rudraksha is used for North-East Direction.

CRYSTAL THERAPY

In this section, we have provided a list of gems and crystals which can be used as a remedy for different directions.

- Yellow Jade in North-East Direction
- Yellow Aventurine in North-East Direction
- Yellow Jasper in North-East Direction
- Yellow Garnet in North-East Direction
- Citrine in North-East Direction
- Yellow Tourmaline in North-East Direction
- Yellow Topaz in North-East Direction
- Yellow Opal in North-East Direction
- Yellow Labradorite in North-East Direction
- Yellow Agate in North-East Direction
- Orange Sunstone in East Direction
- Orange Topaz in East Direction
- Orange Tourmaline in East Direction
- Orange Garnet in East Direction
- Orange Opal in East Direction
- Orange Sphalerite in East Direction
- Orange Flourite in East Direction
- Carnelian in East Direction
- Orange Agate in East Direction
- Peach Aventurine in East Direction

- Orange Citrine in East Direction
- Amber in East Direction
- CZ in South-East Direction
- Asphetic in South-East Direction
- White Topaz in South-East Direction
- Carnelian in South Direction
- Red Garnet in South Direction
- Red Jasper in South Direction
- Red Agate in South Direction
- Red Fluorite in South Direction
- Smokey Quartz in South-West Direction
- Bronzite in South-West Direction
- Brown Agates in South-West Direction
- Grey Agates in South-West Direction
- Tiger's Eye Crystal in South-West Direction
- Amber in South-West Direction
- Smokey Topaz in South-West Direction
- Lapis Lazuli in West Direction
- Hematite in West Direction
- Angelite in West Direction
- Black Obsidian in West Direction
- Blue Tourmaline in West Direction
- Aquamarine in West Direction
- Blue Agate in West Direction
- Black Agate in West Direction
- Iolite in West Direction
- Sodalite in West Direction
- Blue Fluorite in West Direction
- Blue Amber in West Direction
- Azurite in West Direction
- Black Opal in West Direction
- Black Pearl in West Direction
- Black Onyx in West Direction
- Black Tourmaline in West Direction

- Kyanite in West Direction
- Clear Quartz in North-West Direction
- White Agate in North-West Direction
- White Jade in North-West Direction
- Natural Pearl in North-West Direction
- Mother of Pearl in North-West Direction
- Moonstone in North-West Direction
- Green Jade in North Direction
- Green Aventurine in North Direction
- Green Agate in North Direction
- Green Garnet in North Direction
- Green Tourmaline in North Direction
- Peridot in North Direction
- Hiddenite in North Direction
- Green Amber in North Direction
- Green Turquoise in North Direction
- Malachite in North Direction
- Green Fluorite in North Direction
- Green jasper in North Direction
- Amazonite in North Direction
- Florite in North Direction
- Green Tourmaline in North Direction

ASTRO-COLOR THERAPY

In this section, we have provided a list of colors representing different directions, which can be used as a remedy.

- Green Color – North Direction – Planet Mercury Mars
- Yellow Color – North-East Direction – Planet Jupiter
- Orange Color – East Direction – Planet Sun
- Silver & Sparkling White Color – South-East Direction – Planet Venus
- Red – South Direction – Planet Mars
- Brown & Grey – South-West Direction – Planet Rahu
- Black & Blue Color – West Direction – Planet Saturn
- Pearl White Color – North-West Direction – Planet Moon

- Greenish Yellow or Yellowish Green – Between North & North East Direction – Planet Ketu

ASTRO-NUMEROLOGY

In this section, we have provided a list of numbers which can be used as a remedy for different directions.

- North-East Direction – Numbers 9 & 12
- East Direction – Number 5
- South-East Direction – Numbers 2 & 7
- South Direction – Number 8
- South-West Direction – Numbers 1, 10 & 11
- West Direction – Numbers 1, 10 & 11
- North-West Direction – Number 4
- North Direction – Numbers 3 & 6

PYRAMIDOLOGY

In this section, we have provided various methods on how to apply pyramids as a remedy for different vastu doshas and directions.

- Place 9 pyramids in the ceiling of the Bhrahmasthan upside down
- Place 9 pyramid chips under the floor or tiles of the Bhrahmasthan of the house
- Place 9 pyramid chips under the tiles of Bhrahmasthan of each room
- Place 9 pyramids chips in the Bhrahmasthan of the wall of that room
- Use 3, 6, 9 pyramids in extension corners
- Use 3, 6, 9 pyramids in cutout corners
- Place 9 x 3 = 27 pyramids at the entrance of the gate – 9 in top center, 9 in left side & 9 in right side
- If there is any beam or wall on Bhrahmasthan, then place 3 pyramids with foundation / neevon ki samagri in it at the end of the wall or at any place at Bhrahmasthan
- If there are stairs at the Bhrahmasthan, then put foundation / neevon ki samagri in Bhrahmasthan &

place 9 / 18 / 27 pyramids around the pillar to cover almost all the visible sides of pillar / beam. We can use 9+3 / 9+6 / 18+3 / 18+6 / 27+3 / 27+6, denominations also to cover the visible directions

- If there is toilet in Bhrahmasthan, then put foundation samagari (Neevon ki Samagri) & 3, 6, 9 pyramids on the outside & inside of the entrance
- If there is kitchen or any water element in Bhrahmasthan, then place 9 pyramids on the entrance of the inside & outside of the kitchen
- If there is kitchen in north-west direction or air element, then place 3 pyramids on the above of the cooking gas stove / chula
- If kitchen is in earth element or south, south-west direction, then place 9 pyramids on the south-east direction / Bhrahmasthan of the kitchen / center of the wall
- If toilet is in front of the kitchen or attached wall to wall to the kitchen, then attach / place / put / install 9 pyramids at the entrance of both if they are facing each other & if attached wall to wall then put 9 pyramids on that wall of the kitchen
- If want to activate health of the whole family, then place 9 pyramids in the kitchen & 9 pyramids in the Bhrahmasthan
- If entrance is not in right pada or grid, then place 9 + 9 pyramids inside & outside of the entrance or at side walls of the main door
- To protect your house place bagua mirror on the top of the gate / door
- For best fortune / power remedy of entrance, place 9 + 9 + 9 pyramids each on 2 sides & on the top of the door of the entrance
- For bedroom Doshas, place 9 + 9 + 9 + 9 pyramids under your bed in all 4 directions of the bed
- Power remedy for stairs, place 1 pyramid each on both sides of every step on the stairs

- Bed should have small 9 x 9 pyramids at the back or at the resting side, where we sit with our back-touching the bed
- Try to place pyramid in the opposite direction of a room to harmonize the aura & energy around
- To activate & harmonize a dwelling by pyramid vastu, place pyramids in every room, in the dimensions of 1, 3, 6, 9, 12, 15, 18, 21, 24, 27 etc. & so on
- For all extensions & cutouts, minimum 9, 18 or 27 pyramids should be used to balance the negativity
- For all corners, irregular shapes & plots take the square from the shape & treat rest of the area with pyramids to get rid of vastu dosha & harmonize the environment
- Place 9 pyramids if the slope is on the wrong side. Place 9 + 9 pyramids on both sides
- A house should have atleast 81 pyramids in total to harmonize it completely. We can give power treatment by adding more to it in the denominations of 1, 3, 6, 9, 12, 15, 18, 21, 24, 27 etc.
- To protect & treat a house / dwelling, one can use a line of pyramids in its whole boundary with a gap of 1 inch, 3 inches, 6 inches etc., depending upon the size of the plot & size of the pyramids
- To bifurcate any harmful effect of something placed in a dwelling, one can use a bifurcation line of pyramids in between to give protection to the other end from harmful vibrations / energy pattern. But pyramids placed here should always be in the multiple of 9, i.e. 9, 18, 27, 36, 45, 54, 63, 72, 81, and 90 etc.
- Place in multiples of 9, pyramids over / under any heavy object not installed at the right direction. This will cut the negativity / vastu dosha due to

THE GREAT BIBLE OF "REMEDIAL VASTU"

wrong placement of heavy material / objects in the wrong direction
- For servants' quarter, basements, balconies, garage, terrace, overhead water tanks, etc. placing the pyramids in 9 x 9 denominations will give results
- Use pyramids in the basement on the walls & on the ceiling but with precautions
- To block negative energies, using 9 pyramids can create a divide. And to activate that direction, *Vastu Tree's Special Activation Pyramid*s can kick start the positive energies in that direction
- Use 81 pyramids to activate whole plot
- Use *Vastu Tree's Special Colored Pyramids* for all types of directional remedies in the denominations of 3, 6, 9, 12...81 & a *Vastu Tree's Special Power Grid Matrix Construction of Pyramids* to enhance & multiply the positive energies
- Use colored pyramids in special way along with crystals to clear & ward off vastu Doshas
- Use *9 Special Colored Vastu Tree Pyramids* for rectification of sharp corners, unwanted objects, roads, high rise buildings, motor vehicles, Tijori / locker / safe boxes & for Mandir & temples
- Missing numbers in your date of birth & its connected Pyra Numbers or Astro Numbers also provides solutions to balance your life. Then its connected colors further enhance the remedies. (See our Astro-Numerology & Astro-Color Therapy Section to understand the terms)
- Use Pyra-Yantra specially created by Vastu Tree to place those pyramids on that specific direction the pyramid Yantra is made for
- Always use charged & programmed pyramids otherwise it will not work more than 10%
- There is no minimum & maximum number of pyramids allowed in a dwelling. One can use number of pyra-yantras as well. But over activation

of any direction in a dwelling can lead to defects as well. Hence, balancing of number of pyramids as per the requirements is important.

REMEDY BY YANTRAS

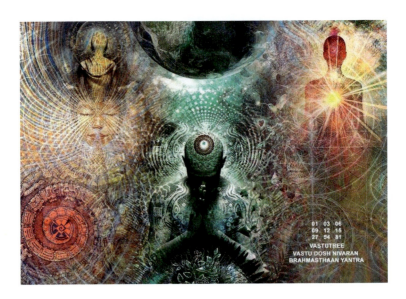

In this section, we have provided a list of yantras which can be used as a remedy for different directions.

- Kuber Yantra – North Direction
- Dhan Yantra – North Direction
- Shri Yantra – North Direction
- Brahaspati Yantra – North-East Direction
- Surya Yantra – East Direction
- Shukra Yantra – South-East Direction
- Yama Yantra – South Direction
- Rahu Yantra – South – West Direction
- Shani Yantra – West Direction
- Chandra Yantra – North-West Direction
- Nav-Grah Yantra
- Vastu Dosh Nivaran Yantra
- Vastu Devta Yantra
- Shree Koorm Yantra
- Bandhan Mukti Yantra

- Matsya Yantra
- Vastu Dosh Nivaran Sudarshan Yantra
- Dikh Dosh Nashak Yantra
- Vastu Tree North Direction Yantra
- Vastu Tree North-East Direction Yantra
- Vastu Tree East Direction Yantra
- Vastu Tree South Direction Yantra
- Vastu Tree South-West Direction Yantra
- Vastu Tree West Direction Yantra
- Universal Yantra

NATURAL REMEDIES

In this section, we have provided a list of natural remedies which can be used for different directions.

- Bach Flower
- Haldi ke Ganesh
- Parad Shivling
- Dhan ka Bandha
- Rudrakshas
- Tulsi
- Chakras Spray
- Meditation Spray
- Relaxation Spray
- Protection Spray
- Shielding Spray
- Cleanser Spray
- Healers Spray
- Anti-stress Spray
- Grounding Spray
- Crystals

- Gems
- Money Plant
- Fish Aquarium
- Place Water Flowing Show Piece in North-East Direction, East Direction, West Direction, North Direction
- Place Green Plants in North
- Place Air Purifiers in North-West
- Guggal Dhuni
- Burning Natural Amber
- Sea Corals
- Deep Sea Shells
- Antrikha / Space Stone Antrikha
- Vastu Tree Special Vastu Diviner ^s in all Directions
- Ekadashi Nariyal
- Dakshinavrati Shankh
- Brahmjaal
- Indrajaal
- Camphor
- Placing Geodes in South & South-West
- Colors
- Shaligram
- Moon Rock
- Adopt a Dog as Pet
- Secret Programmed Vastu Diviners
- Specially Formulated Vastu Dosh Nivaran Yantras
- Kale Ghodhe ki Naal
- Secret Programmed Vastu Diviner with Gold Line for Entrance
- Infinity Gems (Faco Crystals)
- Vishnu Chakra Moti
- Combination of 20-140 Vastu Items & Products
- Fully Round Natural Pearl
- Tutmak Stone

- Timi Stone
- Adra Stone
- **Enemy Stone**
- **Conk Stone**
- Qabana Stone
- **Protection Bug Fossil**
- Eagle Stone
- Triphane Gemstone
- Cordierite
- Hiddenite, Parasha, Green Beryl, Green Florite
- Yellow Florspar, Yellow Beryl, Yellow Spodumene, Scapolite, White Beryl
- 22 Mukhi to 28 Mukhi Rudraksha
- 1 Mukhi Trinetra Rudraksha
- 1 Mukhi Jyotir Lingum Rudraksha
- 1 Mukhi Java Rudraksha
- 1 Mukhi Java Rudraksha Gehuaan Dana
- Natural Pearl Blisters
- Parad Shivling
- Shwetark Ganpati
- Haldi ke Ganesh
- Kastoori
- Kamakhya Sindhoor, Kamiya Sindhoor
- Pure Stone Pyramid
- Education Tower
- Water Charging Crystals
- Negativity Cleaning Crystals
- Rahu ki Kaudi
- Naagmani Glowing
- Jungli Kaali Billi ki Jer
- Jungli Suar ka Daant
- Deep Sea Corals
- Deep Sea Shells
- Kaali Billi ki Jer

- Japanese Blue Coral
- Japanese Black Coral
- Money Eggs
- Charam Pashupati Nath Rudraksha

Installation of Tools, Instruments & Devices

In this section, we have provided a list of installation tools, instruments and devices which can be used as a remedy for different directions.

- Air Purifiers in North-West
- Using Aquariums
- Copper Rods
- Crystal Pencils
- Horse in East
- Elephant in South-West
- Hanuman in South
- Love Birds in North-West
- Mandarin Ducks in North-West
- 9 Types of Special Vastu Tree Vastu Diviners for all 9 Directions
- Crystal Bars
- Bagua Mirror
- Pakua Mirror
- Purane Sikke
- Long Standing Geodes
- Wealth Bowl in North & West
- 3 Metal wirings – Consisting of Copper, silver & Gold
- Infinity Symbol in North & West

- Fishes in west, East North & North-East
- Exhaust Fans
- Room Fresheners
- Camphor Lamp
- Salt Lamp
- Pure Asphetic Crystal Balls
- Wind Chimes
- Camphor Crystals
- Sea Salt
- Gangajal Kalash
- OM Symbol
- Swastik Symbol
- Black Horse Shoe
- Convex Mirror
- Concave Mirror
- Plain Mirror
- Various Pyramids to enhance your health, meditation, energies, utility items & to charge food and water, milk, flowers, rechargeable batteries, tea, coffee, etc.
- Education Tower
- Asphetic Pyramid
- Bamboo Plant in North, North-East & West
- Globe in East, Bhrahmasthan & West
- Magnetic Compass
- Picture of Sun
- *Vastu Tree's Special Activation Pyramids*
- *Vastu Tree's Special Colored Pyramids*
- *Vastu Tree's Special Power Grid Matrix Construction of Pyramids*
- *9 Special Colored Vastu Tree Pyramids*
- Pyra-Yantra specially created by Vastu Tree
- Trishul, Swastik & OM combo Symbol or Picture
- Wind chimes with 4 rods in North-West
- Wind Chimes with 3 & 6 rods in North

- Wind Chimes with 5 rods in East
- Wind Chimes with 2 & 7 rods in South-East
- Wind Chimes with 8 rods in South
- Wind Chimes with 10 & 11 rods in South-West & also in West

Therapies

In this section, we have provided a list of different therapies which can be applied as a vastu remedy.

- Picture Therapy
- Agni Therapy
- Mantra Therapy
- Yantra Therapy
- Mirror Therapy
- Crystal Therapy
- Color Therapy
- Music Therapy
- Flower Therapy
- Water Therapy
- Plants Therapy
- Aroma Therapy
- Magnetic Therapy
- Dowsing Therapy
- Spiritual Therapy
- Distant Healing Therapy
- Chakras Therapy
- Astro Travel Therapy
- Tatva Therapy
- Planet Therapy
- Energy Therapy
- Sound Therapy

- Symbol Therapy
- Crystal Grid Therapy

Mantras

In this section, we have provided a list of different mantras which can be used as a vastu remedy.

Deity Name	Mantra
Shikhi (Ish) – North-East	Om Shikye Namah
Parjanya	Om Parjanya Namah
Jayant	Om Jayantay Namah
Indra	Om Kulishayundhay Namah
Surya – East	Om Suryay Namah
Satya	Om Satyay Namah
Brish	Om Brishae Namah
Antariksha (Sky)	Om Akashaye Namah
Anil (Air)	Om Vayave Namah
Pushya	Om Pushay Namah
Vitath	Om Vitathay Namah
Vrihatkshat	Om Vrihatkshatay Namah
Yam – South	Om Yamay Namah
Gadharva	Om Gandharvay Namah
Bhringaraja	Om Bringarajay Namah
Mrig – South-West	Om Mrigay Namah
Pitri	Om Pitre Namah
Dauwarik	Om Dauwarikay Namah
Sugreeva	Om Sugreevay Namah
Pushpadant	Om Pushpadantay Namah
Varun – West	Om Varunay Namah
Asur	Om Asuray Namah
Shesha	Om Sheshay Namah
Papayakshama	Om Papaharay Namah
Roga – North-West	Om Rogaharay Namah
Nag	Om Ahiye Namah
Mukhya	Om Mukhyai Namah
Bhallat	Om Bhalaatay Namah

Som (Kuber) – North	Om Somay Namah
Bhujang (Sarp)	Om Sarpay Namah
Aditi	Om aditaye Namah
Diti	Om Ditaye Namah
Aap	Om Aapai Namah
Savitra	Om Savitre Namah
Jaya	Om Jayay Namah
Rudra	Om Rudray Namah
Aryama	Om Aryamay Namah
Savita	Om Savitay Namah
Vivaswan	Om Vivaswate Namah
Vibudhadhip	Om Vibudhadhip Namah
Mitra	Om Mitray Namah
Rajayakshama	Om Rajayakshmyai Namah
Prithvidhar	Om Prithvidharay Namah
Apavatsa	Om Apavatsay Namah
Brahma	Om Brahmay Namah

PART 05

These are Secret Programmed & Specially Formulated Vastu Dosh Nivaran Yantras, Vastu Diviners, Ready to Use Remedial Vastu Kits & Direction Enhancer Kits available by Vastu Guru, Dr. Pankaj Verma.

SECRET PROGRAMMED VASTU KITS
These include various types of kits like:

1. **Basic Vastu Kit** – Containing various combination of vastu healing products & items. Total 120 in number.
2. **Advance Vastu Kit** – Containing various combination of vastu healing products & items. Total 160 in number.
3. **Pro Vastu Kit** - Containing various combination of vastu healing products & items. Total 200 in number.
4. **All In One Remedial Vastu Kit** - Containing various combination of vastu healing products & items. More than 200 in number.
5. **Geopathic Stress Removal Kits**
6. **Brahma-Sthaan Dosh Nivaran (Defect Correction) Kit**

SECRET PROGRAMMED DIRECTION ENHANCER KITS
These include various types of directional enhancers, which can be used in Combination with Basic / Advance / Pro / All in One Vastu Kits, to enhance the power of specific directions and its purpose.

1. **Enhancer Kit for NORTH Direction**
2. **Enhancer Kit for NORTH EAST Direction**

3. Enhancer Kit for WEST Direction
4. Enhancer Kit for SOUTH WEST Direction
5. Enhancer Kit for SOUTH EAST Direction

* Consult Vastu Guru Dr. Pankaj Verma for Right Placement
^ Very Effective Remedy

Contact Details

Dr. PANKAJ VERMA
(Vedic Astrologer, Vastu Shastri, Remedy Expert & Geo-Energy Healer)
Whatsapp: +91-8882222333
Email: p.1818@yahoo.com
Web: www.vastutree.com |
www.powervastu.com

FOUNDER OF:
- Bifurcating Line of Vastu
- Astro-Numerology
- Astro-Color Therapy
- Sampoorna Vastu Dosh Nivaran Kits
- Geopathic Stress Removal Vastu Kits
- Foundation Correction Vastu Kits (Neevon ki Samagri)
- Directional Healing Vastu Kits
- Specially Formulated Vastu Dosh Nivaran Directional Power Yantras

Our Specialisations

- Astrology Consultation (Kundali)
- Remedial Astrology (Upaye)
- Vastu Consultation & Energy Vastu
- Vastu Remedies without Demolition
- Angel Card Reading Consultation
- Astro-Numerology Consultation
- Vastu & Other Occult Courses

Our Products

- Remedial Vastu Kits, Vastu Healing Tools, Geopathic Stress Healing Kits & Sampoorna Vastu Dosh Nivaran Foundation Kits
- Specially Formulated Gemstone Remedy for Profession / Career, Higher Studies, Studies & its related issues
- Specially Formulated Gemstone Remedy for Delay in Marriage & Other Marriage related issues
- Certified Rudrakshas
- Certified Gemstones
- Vastu Products
- Pyramids
- Yantras
- Genuine Spiritual Products
- Parad Products
- Healing Crystals, etc.

NOTE: ALL OUR VASTU HEALING PRODUCTS ARE FULLY CHARGED, ENERGIZED & ACTIVATED FOR MAXIMUM HEALING EFFECTS.

Printed by Amazon Italia Logistica S.r.l.
Torrazza Piemonte (TO), Italy

54132555R00210